THE CROMFORD PEAK RAILWAY

John Marshall

NLR 0-6-T 58860 at the west end of Hopton incline with two water tanks, 5 June 1950 *(W. A. Camwell)*

Published by Martin Bairstow, Fountain Chambers, Halifax, West Yorkshire
Printed by Amadeus Press Ltd, Huddersfield, West Yorkshire
Typesetting by Highlight Type Bureau Ltd, Bradford, West Yorkshire

Introductory Note

In 1981 the Author completed a small book on the Cromford & High Peak Railway which was published by David & Charles Ltd in 1982. At that time this was all that would be undertaken by the publisher on this subject and, as a result, the author was left with a large quantity of unused research material, much of it of great importance and interest. It was the intention from the start that a larger book should be written to use this material and also many interesting photographs that were omitted. Several of these had been kindly provided by W.A. Camwell, H.C. Casserley, Dr J.R. Hollick and E.R. Morten, all of whom are sadly no longer with us. It is hoped that there will be no objection to their being used at last. The author's own active interest in the CHPR dates back only to the late 1930s, and he is grateful to those whose photographic activities extended further back.

Most research was carried out at the Public Record Office at Kew and at the Derbyshire County Record Office at Matlock. Much work on Acts and Parliamentary papers was done at Manchester Public Library. The author is grateful to the staffs of these places; and also for help given by Mr G.J. Aston, Dr A.L. Barnett, Messrs Harold D. Bowtell, Allan Brackenbury, the late Dr J.R. Hollick and Messrs G.O. Holt, P.J. McArthy, Ken Harwood (former warden at Middleton top), Alan Rimmer and Geoffrey Webb. Brian Fawcett, who died in 1984, skilfully produced the wash drawing of the Crewe Goods 2-4-0 on the train leaving the north end of Buxton tunnel entirely from an assortment of photographs.

There is little point in compiling a bibliography, but the following are worth mentioning:

Arkwright Society, Matlock, *The Cromford & High Peak Railway – the early years,* a documents pack, 1980

Aston, G.J., 'Cromford & High Peak Locomotives', *Journal of the Stephenson Locomotive Society* August 1951

Hodgkins, D.J., 'The origins and independent years of the Cromford & High Peak Railway', *Journal of Transport History* Vol 6 No 1, May 1963

'The Cromford & High Peak Railway in 1843', *Journal of the Railway & Canal Historical Society* Vol XXIV No 1 March 1978

'Captain Moorsom and the attempt to revive the Cromford & High Peak Railway', *Derbyshire Archaeological Journal* 1983

Rimmer, A., *The Cromford & High Peak Railway* Oakwood Press, 1956, 1985

Two wagons of limestone starting away from the summit of Middleton incline. *(D.W.K. Jones)*

1. Projection and Opening

In the early nineteenth century the Derbyshire Pennines formed a barrier between the coalfields and agricultural areas of Derbyshire, Nottinghamshire and Leicestershire and the textile mills of Lancashire, as well as to trade between Nottingham and Stockport and Manchester. The region was penetrated by the Cromford Canal, opened in February 1792, which connected Richard Arkwright's industrial establishment at Cromford with the Erewash Canal and the Trent. It was built by William Jessop (1745-1814) who was also engineer to the Trent Navigation, the Grand Junction Canal, West India Docks in London, the Surrey Iron Railway, the Croydon, Merstham & Godstone Railway, Fen drainage, and many other works. He was one of the original partners, with Benjamin Outram, Francis Beresford and John Wright, in the formation of the Butterley Company in 1790.

On the North-west side the Peak Forest Canal was opened to basins at Bugsworth (later Buxworth) and Whaley Bridge on 1 May 1800, giving access from Manchester to the limestone of the Peak District. It was engineered by Benjamin Outram who had worked under William Jessop on the Cromford Canal.

Between the two canals lay a stretch of high limestone country, much of it over 1,200ft above sea level, totally unsuitable for canal construction, although a High Peak Junction Canal was proposed in 1810 and surveyed by John Rennie who estimated its cost at £650,000. Its route from Cromford was to be via Grindleford, Hope and Edale and through a tunnel $2\frac{3}{4}$ miles long to the Peak Forest Canal at Chapel Milton, but it failed because of the great expense. The obvious alternative was a railway.

On Saturday 5 June 1824 notices appeared in newspapers in Nottingham, Derby and Manchester[1] announcing a meeting to be held 'at the house of Mrs Cummings, The Old Bath, Matlock, on Wednesday 16th June at 12 o'clock to consider the expediency of forming a communication between the Cromford and Peak Forest Canals by an iron railway, with a branch to Macclesfield, and to take such steps as may be necessary for carrying the plan into execution'.

Samuel Oldknow (1756-1828), a noted industrialist in the North West and a promoter of the Peak Forest Canal, and then High Sheriff of Derbyshire, chaired the meeting. It was resolved 'That no gentleman from Macclesfield having attended the meeting, the consideration of forming a branch railway to that place be deferred' and that no expense should be incurred until £50,000 had been subscribed.[2] The following were appointed to form a committee for furthering the measure and for carrying the views of the meeting into effect: Peter Arkwright; Thomas Bateman; William Bateman; Thomas Brown; Dr Ewes Coke; Philip Gell; Thomas Gisbourne; G. Goodwin; Philip Heacock; Thomas Holland; Francis Hurt; William Jessop; Edward Lloyd; Samuel Oldkow; John Ryle; any three of whom should be competent to act.

At the next meeting, in Manchester on 28 July 1824, it was reported that the necessary £50,000 had been subscribed. The branch to Macclesfield was to be abandoned. Josias Jessop was appointed engineer. He was born at Fairburn in Yorkshire on 24 October 1781, and was the second son of William Jessop. He had acted as assistant to his father, particularly in the building of the Croydon, Merstham & Godstone Railway, and in the construction of Bristol Harbour; and he was also engineer of the Mansfield & Pinxton Railway in 1817. It was decided at this meeting to ask him to prepare a plan and estimate of the proposed line.

During the following weeks Jessop made a rough survey of the route and prepared a report which was presented at the meeting of the committee of the promoters at the Great Hall, Buxton, on 2 September 1824 under the chairmanship of Samuel Oldknow. Jessop's report, dated Butterley, 1 September 1824, is as follows:[3]

To the Committee of the Promoters of the intended Railway from the Cromford Canal to the Peak Forest Canal.

GENTLEMEN,

In pursuance of your directions, I have examined the Country between the Cromford and the Peak Forest Canals, and have taken the levels for a Railway in the most direct line of communication with them without diverging for the purposes of any local trade, which in fact would not be materially affected by any variation to the East or West; and taking into consideration the elevated, mountainous, and occasionally precipitous district of Country through which it passes, (the summit level of the Railway being a thousand feet above the Cromford Canal, and upwards of eleven miles in length), the line on the whole is exceedingly favourable.

I have drawn a plan of the Country to accompany this Report, which will assist in explaining the course of the Railway; the line is laid down from actual admeasurement, the roads connected with it from Surveys which Mr. Heacock obligingly lent me, and from the general maps of the County, correcting them by my own observations, the general features I ascertained by compass bearings and by sketches taken at the same time, which are sufficiently accurate for the purpose.

The Railway commences at the Canal half a mile distant from Cromford by an Inclined Plane, which attains an elevation of 465 feet, and will pass over the summit of the Road between Cromford and Wirksworth at Steeple House, by an Archway 20 feet higher than the surface of the Road; it proceeds a short distance on a level towards Middleton Cross, where a second inclined Plane is necessary, which rises 265 feet, it then continues on a level to the summit of the Via-Gellia, between Cromford and Hopton, which it must cross by an Archway, when a third Plane of 60 or 70 feet rise and about 3½ miles distant from the commencement of the Railway, reaches an elevation of about 800 feet above the Canal, which may be continued nearly twelve miles, passing Brassington Moor, and on the lowest part of the hill to the left of a high rocky point near Mr. Gregory's of Harbro'; thence more Westerly, over the lowest part of the ridge where the Ashbourn and Bakewell Road passes, between Long Cliff and Straight Knoll; it then inclines more Northerly, leaving the high hill of Mininglow to the right, till it approaches Pike Hall, where the range of high land terminates in a Northerly direction, and it becomes necessary to go Westwardly and embank the valley near Mininglow Farm, and pass between Gotham and Pike Hall; it crosses the Newhaven and Pike Hall, and the Ashbourn and Bakewell roads, leaving Newhaven Inn half a mile to the left, and inclines towards the Manchester Road; when from the gradual rise of the ground, it is necessary (if the same level be preserved) to tunnel about 1400 yards, the lowest part of the range being 75 feet above this level of the Railway; it then proceeds above Custard House and below Mr. Abbot's of Coatsfield, to the Moneyash and Hartington Road, where a fourth Plane attains the summit level of 1000 feet above the Cromford Canal, and 760 above the Peak Forest Canal at Whaley. If a Tunnel of 1400 yards through Limestone should be thought objectionable, it's necessity may be obviated by an additional Plane. The fourth Plane will then take place either near Elkelow Hill or at the hill between Mr. Alsopp's of Burntcliff, and the Manchester Road; and the fifth, to attain the summit near Hurdlow, dividing the ascent of the single Plane with a Tunnel, into two smaller ones without it. From the top of the Plane near Hurdlow the level is continued over the lowest range of ground between Chelmerton Low and Brierlow, on the West side of the Manchester Road. The Railway for 3 or 4 miles passes a rugged and uneven Country to the Axe Edge range of mountains, its course being Westwardly round Brierlow and Hindlow along the rocky hill side near Hillhead, then Northwardly to the Harper Hill Lime-Works, and Westwardly under High Edge, to Dale Head, near Thirkelow Gate, where the Country becomes very favourable and continues so to the end. From Dale Head, the direction is Northwardly along Ladmanlow and Burbage Edge, crossing the deep Gully which divides the two hills, it passes to Edge-End, (at which point the Waters separate, running to the Eastern and Western Seas:) the lowest part of the range of mountain is 1140 feet above the Cromford Canal and is so favourable for a Tunnel, that the depth of 140 feet is passed by one of 500 yards long, through Shale and Coal measures. The summit level is continued through the Tunnel and until it pass the Goyt Road, and is altogether 11¼ miles in length. The Line then descends 460 feet to the valley of the Goyt, by an inclined Plane; and of necessity, from the abruptness of the rise at the foot of the hills, crosses the River Goyt into Cheshire, for a few Chains only. From the bottom of this Plane the level gradually leaves the River on account of the rapid descent of the Valley, and passes along the side of the hill, until it cross the Manchester Road, near Ferneylee, and continues forward to the East of Shallcross Hall, and there descends by a Plane 265 feet into the valley at Horridge. There is a further fall of 45 feet to the Peak Forest Canal at Whaley Bridge, which may be passed either by a short Plane or by continuing the Canal to Horridge Bridge, the Feeder being 15 feet higher than the foot of the Plane; the distance to the Canal is 50 Chains.

I have perhaps been more minute than necessary in describing the course of the Railway, but it will afford information to those Gentlemen, who are locally interested. The Plan will explain to the Committee the causes which make the circuitous course round Buxton unavoidable; yet on the whole the direction of the line is favourable and the distance less than 32 miles.

Although from the irregularities of a mountainous Country, the expense of forming the line will be considerable, on the other hand it abounds with excellent materials for making the Railway. In a survey taken solely with a view of ascertaining the direction of the line, the necessary data are not afforded on which an Estimate can be formed, but I have a feeling amounting almost to conviction, that the sum originally stated (£4,000. per mile on the average) will be sufficient for the purpose, and it may not be improper to add that I have had many years experience in similar works to assist me in forming an opinion.

The Railway is proposed to be constructed on the system of Levels and Inclined Planes, by which Steam Engines may be employed as the moving power to convey the Waggons. The locomotive or travelling Engines being used on the Level Part, and stationary Engines at the Inclined Planes. Railways so constructed, are equally adapted to the employment of Engines or Horses, for on the level parts, the friction of the Wheels of the Locomotive Carriages against the Rails, is sufficient to propel them. As Steam Engines, where the trade is extensive, have many advantages over Horses, conveying at much less cost and with greater expedition, it would be desirable for the committee to obtain powers, to enable the Company of Proprietors, either to be come the Carriers, or agree with Individuals, who may be disposed to embark capital in the waggons and Engines, for that purpose; this is the more necessary, as from the greater velocity with which the steam Engines may travel, Horses and Engines could not use the Railway in common without disadvantage.

In compliance with the wishes of the Committee, I have estimated the probable trade of the Railway. Although such statement can only be considered as an approximation to the truth, it is self-evident that a communication which forms the connecting link to several well established Canals – which shortens the *distance of intercourse between the great manufacturing districts of Lancashire, and of Derbyshire, and Nottinghamshire, and also of the Eastern and Southern Agricultural Counties – which will save time and expense in transport – which will convey as cheaply and with more expedition than a Canal, and be effected at one fourth of the cost – which has in its course valuable Mines and extensive Quarries of Limestone and Gritstone – it is evident (I repeat) that such a communication cannot fail to remunerate amply the Promoters of the measure.*

A few observations are necessary to explain the Grounds from which the amount of some of the Articles of the Estimate is derived. The Population of Lancashire in 1821 was 1,052,859, and must have increased considerably since that period, from the immense increase of manufacturers and trade, and may now be estimated at 1,200,000 which is more than one person to each acre of land, and the average of England being three acres for each person, the subsistence of two thirds of Lancashire must be drawn from other sources; which proportion of its whole annual consumption of Grain is upwards of 400,000 Tons; of this I have supposed a tenth part to pass along the Railway. The amount of Cotton wool annually imported is 80,000 Tons. The produce of sheep's wool 20 years ago was 70,000 Tons and must have increased: of these two Articles some will pass one way and some both, in their raw and their manufactured state. The Coals taken from Cromford exceed 40,000 Tons annually and will of course increase with the greater facility of conveyance. The Hopton Wood stone has hitherto been limited in its sale only by the means of conveying it away, and will become an extensive article of carriage. The large flat Paving Stone which is of excellent quality, and Stone Slates produced at Goyt's Clough Quarries, the Lime-stone, Grit-stone, Minerals, &c. will be very considerable; but without entering further into particulars, I proceed to the Statement deduced from them, which I will call the probable revenue.

PROBABLE REVENUE

	TONS		£
Grain as before stated,	40,000	carried 30 Miles at 2d. per Ton per Mile,	10,000
Coal,	60,000	on the average carried 10 Miles at 1d.	2,500
Lime and Limestone,	10,000	8 Miles at 1d.	333
Paving Stones, Slate, &c.	10,000	30 Miles at 1d.	1,250
Hopton Wood Stone and Gritstone,	5,000	average 20 Miles at 1d.	468
Pig Iron, Bar Iron, and Lead,	4,000	30 Miles at 1d.	500
Timber, Hay, &c.	1,000	30 Miles at 1d.	125
Wool and Cotton (raw,)	2,000	30 Miles at 2d.	500
Nottingham, Derby, and Leicester trade to Manchester and the Neighbourhood	2,000	30 Miles at 2d.	500
Manchester trade to the Southward and Eastward	5,000	30 Miles at 2d.	1,250
Huddersfield and Yorkshire trade,	1,000	30 Miles at 2d.	250
Groceries, Spirits, &c.	1,000	30 Miles at 2d.	250
Sundries as Hops, Cheese, Salt, Earthenware, Dying and Bleaching Goods, Moulding Sand, Provisions and many other Articles,	3,000	30 Miles at 2d.	750
			£18,676
From which deduct the Repairs of 32 Miles of Railway at £30. per Mile,	960		
Agency and Incidental Expenses,	1,040		2,000
Being 11 per Cent. on a capital of £150,000			£16,676

Exclusive of the above rates a charge is intended to be made for the use of the Steam Engines on the Planes and to cover the expense of the cost and maintenance of the Locomotive Engines, all of which may be comprehended under the head "Carriage" and together will not amount to a penny per Ton per Mile.

I have the Honour to be

GENTLEMEN,

Your most obedient Servant,

JOSIAS JESSOP.

BUTTERLEY, 1st. *September*, 1821

It was resolved that Mr Jessop's report was practicable and he was asked to proceed immediately with the plans and estimate for Parliament. Mr Brittlebank was 'to give the regular notice in compliance with the standing orders of the House for that purpose'. During the autumn of 1824 he made a detailed survey of the line and prepared the plan, section and estimate which were presented at the meeting at the Bridgewater Arms, Manchester, on 1 December.

Jessop's second report, dated Butterley Hall 29 November 1824, reads as follows:

To the Committee of the proposed Railway from Cromford to the Peak Forest Canal at Whaley Bridge

GENTLEMEN,

Having completed the Survey of the proposed Railway from Cromford to the Peak Forest Canal at Whaley, and prepared the Plans necessary to enable you to proceed to Parliament in the next Session; I now submit to you the Estimate for a double line, formed from accurate admeasurements, of which the particulars are detailed in the accompanying paper, and the following is an Abstract.

	£.	s.	d.
Common Forming, ...	2319	19	0
Cutting and Banking	17,015	10	8
Facewalling to Embankments, ...	1175	17	0
Bridges and Culverts, ...	1633	10	0
Tunnel at Burbage Edge, ...	5700	0	0
Stoning	7656	0	0
Fencing, ...	6400	0	0
Cast Iron Rails, ...	61,950	0	0
Blocks, Nails, and Laying Down, ...	5810	0	0
Land, ...	4800	0	0
Houses and Compensations, ...	1000	0	0
Wharfs and Warehouses, ...	2000	0	0
Contingencies at 10 per Cent.	11,746	0	0
	£129,206	16	8
Steam Engines, &c. for the Inclined Planes, ...	20,000	0	0
	£149,206	16	8

Although I have made considerable allowance for the advance on Iron and the probable rise of labour, yet the Estimate does not exceed the sum originally stated as the probable expence.

In the direction of the Railway I have not seen reason to make any material alteration from the course described in my former report, but to avoid the necessity of tunnelling through the high ground near Haven Lodge, I have made the Railway ascend an eleventh of an Inch in a Yard after passing the Embankment near Pike Hall, and continued that ascent for 3½ miles which leaves a deep cutting of 24 feet at the brow of the hill; this slight rise will not be attended by any inconvenience, as its obstruction to carriages will not be greater than is caused by the curves of the Railway: it will only require the precaution of laying the curves in this part perfectly level.

As the general opinion of Railways has been formed from those of long standing, and imperfect construction, no public one on the new system being yet completed, their effect and advantages are probably much under-rated, and it may be necessary that I should notice the improvement which has so greatly extended their utility, and given them so decided an advantage over all known modes of conveyance for expedition and economy combined with safety.

Every one is aware of the immense advantages that have accrued to this Kingdom from the introduction of Steam Engines to our Mines and Manufactures, which by giving cheapness and facility to labour, and by enabling one man to direct the power which performs the work of hundreds, has raised the Country to its present distinguished preeminence, – had any one ventured to predict it forty years ago, when these changes were in their infancy, there would have been some reason to disbelieve that so important an effect could be produced by a cause apparently so inadequate; but with the experience of the past, there can scarcely be a doubt that these advantages will extend to our modes of conveyance, as it is only an application of the same principle, the substitution of a cheap and powerful mode of performing labour, in place of a more expensive one.

The mode of conveyance that most nearly assimilates to Railways, is Canals: but to them, the agency of Steam cannot be available, as they are limited to the size of their loads, and as regards utility, to the speed of conveyance; for to draw a load of 40 or 50 tons with double the speed that is now done by one horse, could not be effected on a common Canal by any power that can be applied.

The comparatively small expense of forming Railways will be a cause of extending our resources and finding new channels for capital and industry, that would for ever have been neglected, if there were only the more expensive modes of Roads or Canals to resort to; the first being expensive in the carriage, – the latter in the execution: – but a Railway can, according to circumstances, be made at from a half, to a fourth of the expense of a Canal, and convey goods more cheaply, which would render them lucrative when any other mode would be ruinous.*

The old System of forming Railways, was to make them with a regular inclination, adapted to the natural declivity of the country through which they passed; so that a horse had to perform the labour of ascending as well as overcome the friction of the carriages, (for beyond a very small rise, a locomotive Engine will not work to advantage,) the improvement has been to separate as far as possible, the Mechanical Power from the friction, concentrating the power at fixed points, where by means of stationary Steam Engines applied to

*A Canal to form the same connection as is proposed by the Railway, was estimated in October, 1810, by the late Mr. Rennie, to cost £650,000,

Inclined Planes, the ascents are overcome at once, leaving only the friction and the distance to be done by the Horse or the locomotive Engines. A Railway on this system is therefore equally suited to a mountainous or a level country, and either Horses or Locomotive Engines may be used upon it (though not both with advantage at the same time from their difference of velocity,) the waggons being drawn along by the Locomotive Engine, which derives its motion from the contact and friction of the wheels against the Rails, the wheels being attached directly to the Steam Engine.

Where a Railway is level, the power required to move the waggons is little more than the friction, which is found to amount to about a two hundredth part of the weight to be conveyed; or in other words, a power of one pound applied in the direction of the motion, will draw forward 200lbs. but as this supposes all parts of a Railway to be equally perfect, it is right in practice not to calculate on more than 150lbs.

The power to which a Locomotive Engine can be worked on a level Railway, by the friction of the wheels against the rails, before the wheels slide or revolve without advancing, varies under the circumstances of the weather – when the Rails are wet, the friction is equal to 4-32 parts of the weight and when dry 5-32, but practically a tenth part of the weight only should be calculated on as the effective power. – A Locomotive Engine of 10 Horses power will draw 120 Tons at the rate a draught Horse generally travels, or 50 Tons at the rate of 6 miles in an hour: the Engine requires the attendance of only a man and a boy, at a daily expence of 5s.; the Coals consumed in 10 hours, would be from 20 to 30 Cwt.; therefore the expence altogether would be less than 30s. per day, for which 50 Tons may be conveyed 60 miles in 10 hours, which is less than half a farthing per ton per mile; so that making ample allowance for delays, the return of the empty carriages, the cost and maintenance of the Engines, and providing the Waggons, the expences are altogether inconsiderable. I may here remark that the rate of travelling may be increased to surpass that of Mail Coaches, and that the Locomotive Engine will as readily convey 25 Tons (including its own weight) at the rate of 12 miles an hour as double the weight in twice the time.

It is more than 20 years since the Locomotive Engine, worked simply by the friction of its wheels, was used upon the Myrthyr Tydvil Railway in South Wales; but owing to the Railway being made on the old principle, with a declivity, it had not the advantage that was expected. Its next application, was on the Railway from Mr. Brandling's Collieries near Leeds, where a cogged wheel worked into cogs upon the side of the Railway to propel the waggons, but in this instance the advantage was inconsiderable from the same cause, the ascent of the Railway. It was then introduced among the Newcastle Collieries, and observation soon pointed out that it was most effective, as the Railway approached to a level: where ascents or descents were unavoidable they were obviated by the introduction of inclined planes, up which the loaded waggons were drawn by stationary Engines, or the loaded waggons descending drew up the returning empty ones. Their present degree of perfection has thus been gradually attained, and four or five years experience has fully proved their simplicity, cheapness, and regularity.

On the proposed Railway where the ascent from Cromford by four Inclined Planes is nearly 1000 feet, and the descent to the Peak Forest Canal between 7 and 8 hundred feet, by three others, the average cost of working each plane will be about a halfpenny per ton.

When these very moderate expences of carriage are considered, it furnishes an additional argument in favour of the opinion I expressed in my former Report, that a Railway forming so important a connection between rich and populous districts, and with Canals which yield an abundant revenue, cannot be a speculation of hazard, but must be a secure and lucrative mode of investing capital.*

I have the Honour to be
Gentlemen,
Your most obedient Servant,
JOSIAS JESSOP.
BUTTERLEY HALL, Nor. 29, 1824

*The proposed Railway will form a direct communication between the great manufacturing district of Manchester and the manufacturing districts of Derby, Nottingham, and Leicester.

Because of bad weather Jessop was unable to complete the plans and sections and books of reference in time for them to be deposited with the Clerks of the Peace for Derbyshire, at Chesterfield, and Cheshire at Chester. They were deposited by 31 December and, apparently, the rules proved sufficiently flexible for the matter to proceed for the 1825 session of Parliament, for which purpose Mr Brittlebank, the company's solicitor, was obtaining consents of landowners. He had already secured the signatures of the Duke of Devonshire, Richard Arkwright, Philip Gell, William Evans, MP, William Webster, the trustees of Sir Hugh Bateman, Baronet, and other owners of land over which the railway was to pass.

The report of the next meeting, at the Bridgewater Arms, Manchester, on 1 December 1824 was as follows:

HIGH PEAK STEAM RAILWAY

FROM THE CROMFORD CANAL TO THE PEAK FOREST CANAL, IN THE COUNTY OF DERBY.

At a General Meeting of the Committee and Supporters of this Undertaking, held at the time and place above mentioned, in pursuance of a requisition for this purpose,

THOMAS BATEMAN, ESQUIRE, IN THE CHAIR,

The various resolutions previously entered into, and several communications and letters to the

Committee having been stated and read, and the Plan and Survey of the projected line of the Railway, and Mr. Jessop's second report and estimate having been also read and submitted to the Meeting;

IT WAS RESOLVED, That the Meeting receives with the greatest satisfaction the communication that his Grace the Duke of Devonshire consents to the Railway being made through his Grace's Estates, and most liberally without requiring any remuneration for his Land.

RESOLVED, That from the very clear view taken by Mr. Jessop, of the advantages to be derived from the proposed measure, and the satisfactory explanations given in his Report as to the facility and economy of conveyance by Railways; the Meeting is fully convinced that the proposed Railway will be decidedly the best mode of communication between the two Canals, and productive of advantages not to be obtained by any other means, and therefore strongly recommends the scheme to the support of the public.

It appearing from the estimate that the sum of £130,000. is necessary to complete the Railway, and a further sum of £20,000. for Steam Engines, and that about £70,000. is already subscribed, in shares of £100. by the Noblemen, Gentlemen, and Landowners in the immediate neighbourhood of the proposed Railway.

RESOLVED, That the subscription be now open to the public in general, and that subscriptions be received at the Banking Houses of Sir Peter Pole, Bart. & Co. Messrs. Jones, Loyd, & Co. and Messrs. Smith, Payne, and Smiths, in London; and at the several Banks in Liverpool, Manchester, Birmingham, Macclesfield, Derby, Nottingham, Leicester, Stamford, and Lincoln, and that the respective Bankers be requested to receive Subscriptions on account of Messrs. Arkwright, Toplis, & Co. of Wirksworth, Derbyshire, the Treasurers to the Undertaking; and that subscribers do at the time of entering their names, in pursuance of a former resolution, pay the sum of One Pound per Cent. on the amount of their Subscriptions.

RESOLVED, That publicity be given to these Resolutions by insertion in such of the public journals as the Committee may deem necessary, and that Mr. Jessop's Second Report be printed for circulation.

That this Meeting be adjourned to Thursday the 6th January next, at the Old Bath, Matlock, at Eleven o'clock in the forenoon.

(SIGNED,)

THOS. BATEMAN, CHAIRMAN

The thanks of the Meeting were given to the Chairman, for his efficient conduct in the Chair.

BRITTLEBANK & SON, SOLICITORS,
Oddo, Derbyshire.
N.B. The Subscriptions immediately after the Meeting were increased to £130,000

At a meeting at Matlock on 31 January 1825 the committee resolved that the plan for the engine house at the top of the first incline from the Cromford Canal should be approved by Mr Peter Arkwright 'so as to render it as little objectionable to him as possible'. The Cromford & High Peak Railway Company was incorporated by Act on 2 May 1825[4] with powers to construct a railway or tram road from the Cromford Canal near Cromford to the Peak Forest Canal at Whaley (Bridge). The Act authorized the use of stationary and locomotive steam engines, and gave power to raise capital of £164,400 in shares, and loans of £32,880.

Contracts were let during 1826. A longitudinal section of the line, corresponding to that with the deposited plan of 1824, from which the constructed line differed in many places, has been preserved in Derbyshire County Record office.[5] It carries the names of the contractors, as follows:

Cromford & High Peak

RAILWAY

THE REMAINING LOTS

OF THIS RAILROAD,

TO BE

Let by Ticket,

At Newhaven House,

IN THE COUNTY OF DERBY, ON

Wednesday, 14th June, 1826,

AT ONE O'CLOCK IN THE AFTERNOON,

The Roadway & Deep-Cutting,

AND FORMING THE

INCLINED PLANES,

Commencing on Hopton Moor to the Mininglow contract; and from Parsley-Heys, near Newhaven Lodge by Cotes-field, Cronkstone Grange, Hurdlow & Brierlow, to Hindlow Gate above Sterndale, and thence to Hill-end-gate; the same to be divided into Seven or more Lots to suit the convenience of Contractors.

SECTIONS and SPECIFICATIONS may be seen at Newhaven House: at the Duke of York Public House, on the Buxton and Ashborne Turnpike Road: and at the Committee Room, in Cromford: where, and at MR. HOLLAND'S, in Buxton, the Lots will be explained. The Tenders for each Lot to be made at so much per Cube Yard, and also per Rood forward, and to state the time for completing the Lot.

N.B. No Ticket will be received unless sealed and tendered before Twelve o'clock.

By order of the Committee.

BRITTLEBANK AND SON,

Oddo, 1st June, 1826. Clerks to the Company.

PRINTED BY HEMROSE, HOLMES, AND CO., WIRKSWORTH.

Advertisement for contractors, 1826

List of CHPR contractors from a section corresponding to the deposited plan of 1824

Section	Length Miles	Furlongs	Yards	Contractor
Cromford Wharf to bridge over Middleton Road, mile $1\frac{3}{4}$, including Cromford Inclines	1	6	$38\frac{1}{2}$	John Hodgkinson
To Middleton Top, mile $2\frac{5}{8}$ including Middleton incline		6	125	Higgotts & Hollis
To Hopton Foot, mile $3\frac{7}{8}$, including Hopton tunnel	1	2	23	Higgotts & Hollis
To Harbro House, mile $4\frac{7}{8}$, including Hopton incline	1	0	$6\frac{1}{2}$	Staley & Co
To mile $6\frac{1}{3}$ near Longcliffe	1	2	198	Dakin & Co
To Daisy Bank, mile $7\frac{1}{2}$	1	1	15	Dakin & Co
To mile $9\frac{3}{4}$ beyond Minninglow including stone embankments	2	2	0	Milner & Co
To mile $12\frac{7}{8}$ near Friden	32	1	103	Porteous & Co
To mile $14\frac{1}{8}$ near Parsley Hay including Newhaven Tunnel	1	1	154	Porteous & Co
To Hurdlow Foot, mile $16\frac{1}{4}$	2	0	44	Raynor & Co
To mile $17\frac{7}{8}$ including Hurdlow incline	1	3	176	Raynor & Co
To mile $19\frac{1}{4}$ near Dowlow	1	5	0	Raynor & Co
To mile 21 near Hillhead	1	5	145	Taylor & Co
To mile $21\frac{1}{2}$		4	97	Pitchfork & Co
To mile $23\frac{1}{8}$ near Harpur Hill	1	4	198	Pitchfork & Co
To mile $24\frac{1}{4}$	1	1	44	Wardle & Co
To mile 25, Ladmanlow		6	0	Porteous & Co
To mile $26\frac{1}{4}$ beyond Macclesfield Old Road	1	2	0	Bagshaw & Co
To mile $27\frac{1}{4}$ including Buxton tunnel	1	3	44	Upton & Co
To Bunsall Top, mile $28\frac{3}{8}$		5	132	Upton & Co
To Bunsall Foot, mile $29\frac{1}{8}$		5	134	Upton & Co
To mile $30\frac{1}{8}$ at Fernilee	1	0	22	Upton & Co
To Shallcross Top, mile $31\frac{1}{8}$	1	2	22	Upton & Co
To Whaley Bridge canal basin, mile $32\frac{3}{4}$, including Shallcross and Whaley inclines	1	2	59	Upton & Co

(1 Furlong = 220 yd, 8 Furlongs = 1 mile)

Construction had already begun when, on 30 September 1826, Josias Jessop died aged barely 45, following an illness supposedly from over exertion on the railway. He had also been active as a consultant on the Newcastle & Carlisle Railway, and as an engineer on the Liverpool & Manchester Railway where George Stephenson openly regarded his death as the removal of an obstacle to his own progress.[6] He was succeeded by Thomas Jackson Woodhouse who at the time was working as resident engineer under Josias Jessop. Woodhouse was born in Warwickshire on 9 December 1793. His father, John, under whom he was trained, was also a civil engineer as also was his grandfather. He worked on the Grand Junction and the Worcester & Birmingham canals, both including long tunnels. In 1825 he worked with Josias Jessop on a survey for a railway from Birmingham to Bristol.

On 15 November 1827 the *Derby Reporter* published a progress report stating that more than half of the CHPR was

'formed and stoned ready for laying down the blocks and rails permanently. Many of the heavy cuttings which are principally through limestone are completed, and with the exception of the stupendous excavation on Hopton Moor (which is scarcely equalled by anything of the kind in the Kingdom), and the tunnel near Buxton, the whole will be formed next summer. Those works, at the speed they are now being carried on, will be finished in less than two years. A great portion of the masonry has been done during the last season; ten substantial bridges have been built over public roads, exclusive of many accommodation arches for land owners; the engine houses for the Cromford inclined plane are being built, and the engines will be got to work and a trade opened on the lower part of the railway in a few months'.

An almost identical report appeared in the *Nottingham Journal* on 17 November and in the *Sheffield Iris* on 20 November. The *Nottingham Journal* published a further report on 19 December 1829 stating

'The tunnel, between 600 and 700 yards long, near Buxton is in a forward state ... but there remains a considerable quantity of earth to be removed Completion is expected next spring'.

The track, which was of standard 4ft $8\frac{1}{2}$in gauge, consisted of cast-iron fish-bellied rails, 4ft long, 6in deep in the centre and 3in at the ends, laid on stone blocks. These, mostly from Derbyshire millstone grit, measured approximately 17in long, $11\frac{1}{2}$in wide and 8in deep. They were laid with the length at right angles to the rails. A $1\frac{1}{2}$in diameter hole 4in deep, in the centre of the upper surface held an oak plug into which was driven an iron spike to hold down the foot at one end of each rail. The foot contained a socket into which the knuckle end of the adjacent rail fitted. This type of rail was designed by William Jessop in 1792, and he used it on the railway from Nanpantan to Loughborough in 1793-4. Jessop's association may have influenced its use on the CHPR, despite its by then known unsuitability for locomotives. Although more suitable rails of wrought iron had been in use since about 1808, the Butterley Company was unable to supply them. This dependence on the Butterley Co put the CHPR to much additional expense in early replacement of track.

An advertisement for tenders for 500 tons of rails appeared on 18 August 1825. 'The rails to be four feet long and weigh seventy-four pounds each, and to be cast of strong grey iron from Iron Models to be furnished by the Company. – A pattern Rail may be seen at the Greyhound, Cromford, Newhaven House, and the Eagle, Buxton'. Tenders were to be addressed to Brittlebank & Son, Oddo near Wirksworth, by 14 September.

The contract was awarded to the Butterley Company who also supplied 3ft long rails which were used in sidings. The economy of these could not have been great because they used 25 per cent more stone blocks. The 4ft rails cost just under 5 shillings each and weighed about 84.5lb. In a total length of 33 miles 54 chains, 28 miles 47 chains was single line. Double-line sections, amounting to 5

CHPR cast-iron fish-bellied rails in the workshop at Cromford, 12 June 1982
(John Marshall)

miles 7 chains included the inclines which totalled 3 miles 78yd. To lay the main line alone required about 102,300 rails costing about £25,575.

There were seven inclines, listed below, of which two, Cromford/Sheep Pasture and Bunsall Upper and Lower, were originally worked in two sections.

	Incline	Length,yd	Rise or fall,ft	Gradient
1	Cromford	580	204	1 in 8½
2	Sheep Pasture	711	261	1 in 8¼
		1,291	465	
3	Middleton	708	253	1 in 8½
4	Hopton	457	98	1 in 14
5	Hurdlow	850	160	1 in 16
6	Bunsall Upper	660	266	1 in 7½
7	Bunsall Lower	455	191	1 in 7
		1,115	457	
8	Shallcross	817	240	1 in 10½
9	Whaley Bridge	180	40	1 in 13½

For working the inclines the Butterley Co supplied nine twin beam engines. Hopton and Hurdlow inclines were each equipped with an engine producing 20hp and the others, except Whaley incline, 40hp. All the engines except Whaley Bridge were supplied in 1829 and erected in 1829-30. On 1 October 1829 Thomas Woodhouse issued a report on the progress of the works which is worth quoting as it gives a good idea of the extent of the excavation required.[7]

'I shall begin my description of the line at the Cromford end. The railway begins at the Cromford Canal, one mile south of Cromford, and immediately ascends by two inclined planes to an elevation of 465 feet, the lower one being 580 yards long rises 204 feet; the upper one 711 yards long rises 261 feet. The waggons are conveyed up these inclined planes by steam engines, two at each station, of twenty horse-power (or forty horse-power to each plane); and by means of endless chains, directed and supported by pullies, two waggons are conveyed at a time, each containing from five to six tons, and with a velocity of four miles an hour. These are already completed, and have been tried, although not opened for trade. In this length 123,000 cubic yards of excavation have been made, principally through grit or freestone rock, of excellent quality for building purposes. From the top of the second plane, the railway proceeds on a level for rather more than one mile, when it again ascends by the Middleton inclined plane, which rises 253 feet in 708 yards. This part is completed, having had 32,000 cubic yards of excavation done through solid limestone rock; the greatest depth of the cutting being 43 feet. This plane will also be worked by two steam engines of twenty horse-power each similarly applied with the former; they are at present erecting, and will be completed in two months. It then proceeds on a level, and at the further distance of one mile commences the most extensive piece of excavation in the whole line, which has been made principally in the limestone rock, and to the depth of 68 feet. A tunnel through the rock, of 105 yards in extent, (a portion of which is arched masonry), occupies the centre of these cuttings; this work is nearly completed: the material from the cutting, amounting to 169,000 cubic yards, forms the Via Gellia embankment, which immediately adjoins the cutting. At the termination of the embankment, the Hopton inclined plane commences, which rises 98 feet in 457 yards; the two engines for this plane are each of ten horse-power, and are now being erected.

The railway then proceeds for twelve miles, upon a level, with the exception of about two miles, which have a rise of 10 feet in a mile, for the purpose of lessening the depth of a very considerable cutting near Haven Lodge. The principal cuttings in this length are, on Carsington Pasture 20,000 cubic yards; in Brassington liberty, 58,000; to form the

Cromford wharf, June 1940
(John Marshall)

Underbridge at GR 304562, Sheep Pasture incline, 9 March 1992 *(John Marshall)*

Shallcross yard and derelict Shallcross incline, from Chapel en le Frith road bridge, 19 March 1956
(Harold D Bowtell)

Top of Sheep Pasture incline, June 1940 *(John Marshall)*

large embankment at Minninglow, 78,000 yards; and at Pike Hall and Burntcliff 40,000 yards. The extensive cutting near Manchester Road and Haven Lodge, 125,000 cubic yards, and thence to the Hurlow inclined plane 38,000 yards have been excavated. The greater portion of these cuttings have been made through limestone rock, and have been blasted with gunpowder; and the material applied in the formation of embankments. Thus far completes a distance of sixteen miles, on which the rails will be laid, and the road opened for trade by the end of the present year.

The railway then ascends to its summit, or greatest elevation, 168 feet in 850 yards, at the Hurdlow inclined plane, which is formed and ready for the reception of the rails. The engine-house is in preparation for two engines of ten horse-power each. The railway then continues on a level for nearly twelve miles, the greatest of which is prepared for the laying down of the rails. The principal excavations in this length are at Hurdlow and Brierlow, 57,000 cubic yards; at Hindlow 26,000; at Hillhead and Harpurhill, 44,000; and south of Turncliffe, 46,000 yards, all through limestone rocks; north of Turncliffe, 47,000 cubic yards, through shale and clay; also at Ladmanlow and Burbage, 62,000 yards; all these are completed.

The tunnel near Buxton will be 580 yards long, of which 80 yards remain to be executed. The tunnel is 21 feet wide and 16 feet high above the surface of the railway. It has been driven from the ends, without any pit or shaft being sunk, which has protracted the work, and measures passed through have been exceedingly hard clunch or shale, to remove which blasting by gunpowder has been necessarily resorted to. The whole of this tunnel is arched with masonry. It will be completed by the end of the present year. Beyond that tunnel to the Upper Goyt inclined plane, 38,000 cubic yards have been excavated. The Upper Goyt inclined plane descends 266 feet in 660 yards of length: and the lower plane descends 191 feet in 455 yards, which brings the railway into the valley of the River Goyt. These planes, having 30,000 yards of excavation, are formed, and both the engine houses are in considerable forwardness. They will each contain two engines of twenty horse-power, with machinery similar to those before mentioned.

The railway then proceeds on a level for 2¼ miles, having 74,000 cubic yards of cutting in the length, which is nearly completed. Then commences the Shallcross inclined plane, which is 817 yards long and descends 240 feet, the 'forming' being completed, and the engines, two of twenty horse-power each, are in progress. The line forwards is also completed, having 18,000 cubic yards of cutting to the Whaley inclined plane, which is 180 yards long, and falls 42 feet, at the foot of which the railway communicates with the Peak Forest Canal.

After much inquiry and examination into the subject, cast-iron rails have been adopted in preference to the malleable ones, from a belief that they will be found more durable from their construction, more firmly seated on their beds, and readily adjusted; and from their inflexibility, offering less resistance to the movement of the carriages. The rails are cast in lengths of four feet, having the pedistal at one end, and the opposite end adapted to it, to admit of movement at the joining, and at the same time ensure the steadiness of the rail. Each rail weighs 84lbs, or 100 tons of rails are required for a mile of single road.

The total length of the railway is nearly 33 miles, which will be completed and opened for general trade in the course of the ensuing summer. Forty-

seven bridges and archways have been built, three others with cast-iron arches are nearly completed, and two others are in progress; in all fifty-two.

The forming and completing the railway with a double line of road will have cost 150,000 l., and the engines, reservoirs, and machinery, a further sum of 30,000 l.,. making the total outlay of capital 180,000 l., a sum by no means great, when compared with the magnitude of the work, and the many natural obstacles which had to be overcome. In the execution of the work the greatest economy has been observed, although proper care has been taken to effect it in a substantial and permanent manner, utility more than ostentation having governed the Committee in the application of the capital expended.

In concluding, I ought to state, that the Cromford and High Peak Railway was planned and laid out by the late Jos. Jessop, Esq., civil engineer, who unfortunately has not lived to see the completion of it.

I am, Sir, &c.&c.

THOMAS WOODHOUSE.

The malleable iron referred to is cast iron with a low silicon content and is less brittle than ordinary cast iron. No doubt Woodhouse was correct in his reasoning in favour of harder cast iron; but wrought iron, as used on the Liverpool & Manchester Railway would have been better.

It could be asked at this stage why Jessop, in his survey in 1824, did not carry the line down through Buxton and by the course taken later by the Buxton extension of the Stockport, Disley & Whaley Bridge Railway to the terminus at Whaley Bridge, thereby avoiding the Bunsall and Shallcross inclines. Railway engineering was then still in the period of transition from canals and early tramroads. Horses and the primitive locomotives were unable to haul heavy loads on gradients steeper than about 1 in 300. So the early railways were laid out like canals with long level stretches; large changes in elevation were overcome by inclined planes which took the place of locks. It was not until the 1840s that engineers gained confidence in the ability of locomotives to ascend steeper gradients.

The inclines were worked at first by endless chains. On the Hopton, Hurdlow and Whaley inclines chain working survived to the end, but on the others the chains were replaced by hemp ropes in 1855-7. Chains were made in the workshop at Cromford from 3/4in chain iron mostly supplied by Pritt & Co of Liverpool.

Material such as rails and smaller stationary engine parts and castings from the Butterley Co were lowered by a steam crane at the works down a shaft about 100ft deep into boats on the Cromford Canal in the middle of the Butterley tunnel. Larger ironwork was taken down a railway to a wharf at the eastern end of the tunnel. The railway was certainly in operation in 1828[8]. The boats were then legged through the 1 mile 1206yd long tunnel.

As might be expected of a line across such rough upland country, there were considerable engineering works. The route followed contours as far as possible, and so had some sharp curves.

The 5¼ miles from Longcliffe to Friden included 21 curves of 5 chains radius or less; three were 3ch and the sharpest, Gotham, was 2½ ch. It turned through 80° and once had a super elevation of 11in which must have been excessive for the 5mph speed restriction over it. It was these curves, with the cast-iron rails, which made the line unsuitable for locomotives until the rails had been replaced by wrought iron. Curves consisted 4ft straights separated by wide obtuse angles. The outer rails

Foot of Middleton incline, 1941. On the right is the branch to Middle Peak quarry above Wirksworth *(John Marshall)*

were constantly being subjected to sideways pressure and, being weak laterally, they broke. Spurs and valleys had to be crossed by cuttings and embankments. Near Minninglow were two impressive stone-faced embankments, and there were others elsewhere. Three tunnels were required: Hopton 113yd; Newhaven 51yd; and Buxton, generally known as Burbage tunnel, originally 580yd and later extended at the north end. Hopton tunnel was originally about 2yd longer at the Middleton end.

In 1829 plans were deposited for a Stockport Junction Railway to connect the CHPR to the Liverpool & Manchester Railway which was then under construction. The line was to leave the L & M at the Liverpool Road terminus in Manchester and pass through Hulme, Burbage, along the Mersey valley, through Stockport, Lower Marple and New Mills to Whaley Bridge. No Act was obtained and the project was abandoned.

On completion of the railway Woodhouse resigned. In 1832 he was appointed engineer of the Dublin & Kingstown Railway; later he worked on the Midland Counties and other lines. With Brassey and Mackenzie in France he worked on the Rhone – Marne canal. While working in Italy he was suddenly taken ill and died in Turin on 26 September 1855 aged 61. His place on the CHPR was taken by John Leonard who was appointed engineer and manager. Nothing has been found about Leonard, but he served the CHPR with notable efficiency.

The railway was opened in two sections: Cromford Canal to Hurdlow incline foot on 29 May 1830, and from there to Whaley Bridge on 6 July 1831. At first all the traffic was worked by horses between the inclines. The CHPR Co functioned simply as proprietors of the line; traffic was worked by private carriers using their own wagons and horses. A letter dated 6 August 1832 from John Leonard to T.W.Jackson of Mountsorrell, Charnwood Forest in Leicestershire, stressed this fact and explained that German Wheatcroft & Sons would carry stone from Cromford to Manchester at 14 shillings a ton. Also Wheatcroft's boats regularly worked the canals in Leicestershire and could carry stone from there.

A notice in the *Derby Mercury*, 29 May 1833, announced: 'Messrs Wheatcrofts have taken out a licence to convey passengers from Cromford to Whaley, and thence it is presumed a conveyance will be ready to convey them to Manchester'. A paragraph on 15 June 1833 confirmed that the passenger coach was in operation. German Wheatcroft also ran a connecting coach between Whaley Bridge and Manchester. The form of the railway carriage is not known. The service was advertised locally and it never appeared in Bradshaw's Guide.

NOTES

1 *Manchester Chronicle, Manchester Guardian, Nottingham Journal* 5 June 1824
2 *Manchester Chronicle* 19 June 1824
3 Public Record Office (PRO) Kew RAIL 144/6
4 Cromford & High Peak Railway Act 2 May 1825 c 30
5 Derbyshire Record Office (DRO) Gell 58/23b
6 Rolt, L.T.C. *George and Robert Stephenson* 1960 Ch 5 p 115
7 *Companion to the British Almanac* 1830 pp 248-50
8 Riden, Philip, *The Butterley Company 1790-1830* p 20 Author 1973

Top of Middleton incline, June 1940 *(John Marshall)*

Bridge carrying Middleton incline over the Middleton-Wirksworth road, GR 281552, 9 March 1992 *(John Marshall)*

Middleton winding engine, 8 May 1980 *(John Marshall)*

Embankment and bridge near Middleton, GR 275550, 15 May 1980. Stationary engine house on right. *(John Marshall)*

Whaley Bridge basin, Peak Forest Canal, and CHPR wharf from LNWR Buxton line, September 1950
(E.R. Morten)

High Peak Junction
(J.R. Hollick)

LNWR 2-4-0 tank 6428 shunting at High Peak Junction, 14 May 1940
(H.C. Casserley)

2. Traffic

The railway had hardly begun operations when it was threatened with competition. On 9 November 1831 the Macclesfield Canal opened from a junction with the Peak Forest Canal at Marple to a junction with the Trent & Mersey Canal at Kidsgrove, so providing a route between Manchester and Nottingham round the south of the Pennines. The Peak Forest Canal Company allied itself to the CHPR against the Macclesfield and Trent & Mersey companies. Competition led to a reduction of tolls on the canal route from 1d, 1½ and 2d a ton-mile to 1d in April 1841 and to ½d in October. On the CHPR route the Peak Forest Canal Co reduced its toll to 1s a ton throughout from charges ranging from 1s 9d to 3s 6d.

Limestone soon became the predominating traffic over the CHPR and remained so to the end. A letter from Leonard on 20 June 1832 in reply to a complaint by J. Clayton & Son at Marple Ironworks, Cheshire, expresses regret that the quality of the limestone being sent was not satisfactory and that the matter would be raised at the next committee meeting. This suggests that the CHPR had some control over the traffic. On the same day he issued a notice to traders on the railway stating that tonnage must be paid for 'on the first Friday after the end of each month. Traders not paying their tonnage on or before that day will not afterwards be allowed credit'.[1]

To T.W. Jackson of Mountsorrell, Leicestershire, who was wanting to send his stone to Manchester, Leonard wrote as follows on 6 August 1832:

'Your letter respecting the tonnage charges on the CHPR reached me this morning in reply to which I may observe that the Railway Company are not carriers themselves, but merely proprietors of the road. I have, however, made enquiries of one of the carriers, Messrs German Wheatcroft & Sons, who say they will engage to carry the stone from Cromford to Manchester at 14s a ton. They also requested me to say that their boats are regularly plying on the canals in Leicestershire and that they would have no objections to bring the stone from thence.

The CHPR is 33 miles long and extends from the Cromford Canal near Cromford to the Peak Forest Canal at Whaley Bridge. The company's charge on goods passing the entire length is 3s 10½d per ton'.

On 4 September 1832 Clayton at Marple Ironworks was asked for an offer to remove 900-1000 tons of limestone from the wharf at Whaley Bridge. Leonard again wrote to Clayton on 11 October:

'I cannot but regret your having found it necessary to discontinue taking our limestone, particularly as we should soon be able to furnish a regular supply from the Grin quarries'.

The Grin Quarry was close to Ladmanlow, south-west of Buxton. He wrote again on 9 November:

'We can at any time supply as much of the Grin limestone as you mention, but unfortunately, during the suspension of the trade we have nearly filled the wharf with Harpur Hill stone in expectation that when you again commenced you would require something like their 100 tons per week'.

It took more than a year to clear the limestone that had piled up at Whaley Bridge. On 8 October 1832 Leonard wrote to James Meadows, manager of the Peak Forest Canal at Manchester:

'We find on laying the branch into the new warehouse at Whaley that the outside line of rails will in one part come very near to the edge of the feeder, so much so as to prevent the rails and blocks from having sufficient stability. Will you be as good as to give the company directions for something to be done to it to enable the work to be completed?'

The Whaley Bridge warehouse was again the subject of a letter to Meadows on 12 July 1833 stating that Wheatcrofts required another branch from the railway to the opposite side of the warehouse they then occupied.

The problems of working the high section of the railway in winter had already asserted themselves when Leonard wrote to Joseph Glynn at Butterley on 27 October 1832 to tell him that, at a meeting the previous Wednesday, he had been directed to construct a machine for clearing snow. Glynn was chief engineer at the Butterley works. He was later appointed a Fellow of the Royal Society and a Member of the Institution of Mechanical Engineers. He was responsible for the design and manufacture of a large number of early railway bridges and was a pioneer in the application of steam power to land drainage particularly in the Fens where William Jessop had done so much work. It was at the suggestion of William Jessop Junior (c1783-1852), brother of the late Josias and a member of the Butterley Company, that Leonard wrote to Glynn who had a brother at Newcastle well known to the engineers of the Stockton & Darlington Railway. It was hoped they may be able to give advice on a snowplough, but it appears nothing was forthcoming from that direction. Possibly no such machine existed in 1832, for no other railway in Britain reached such an altitude as the CHPR. It would have had to be *pulled* by horses, hardly practicable!

Whaley incline was worked at first by horses, but it was intended to be worked by a stationary engine. At a meeting of the committee on 12 June 1833 it was agreed that the Whaley engine should be erected immediately. Evidently it had been supplied by then. An entry in the Butterley Co ledger on 7 August 1833 read: 'A steam engine 10 horses double power for Whaley Plane ... £600' and on 14 August: 'Brasses and handrail for do ... £9 17 2 Pinions, winding out gear ... £29 4 2' making a total of £639 1 4. This was for a two-cylinder engine of a total of 10hp. On 15 June Leonard wrote to James Meadows Jr, manager of the Peak Forest Canal at Manchester, about the water supply to the engine, asking if the feeder to the Peak Forest Canal might be used, and explaining that the water would be returned to the feeder, which suggests it was a

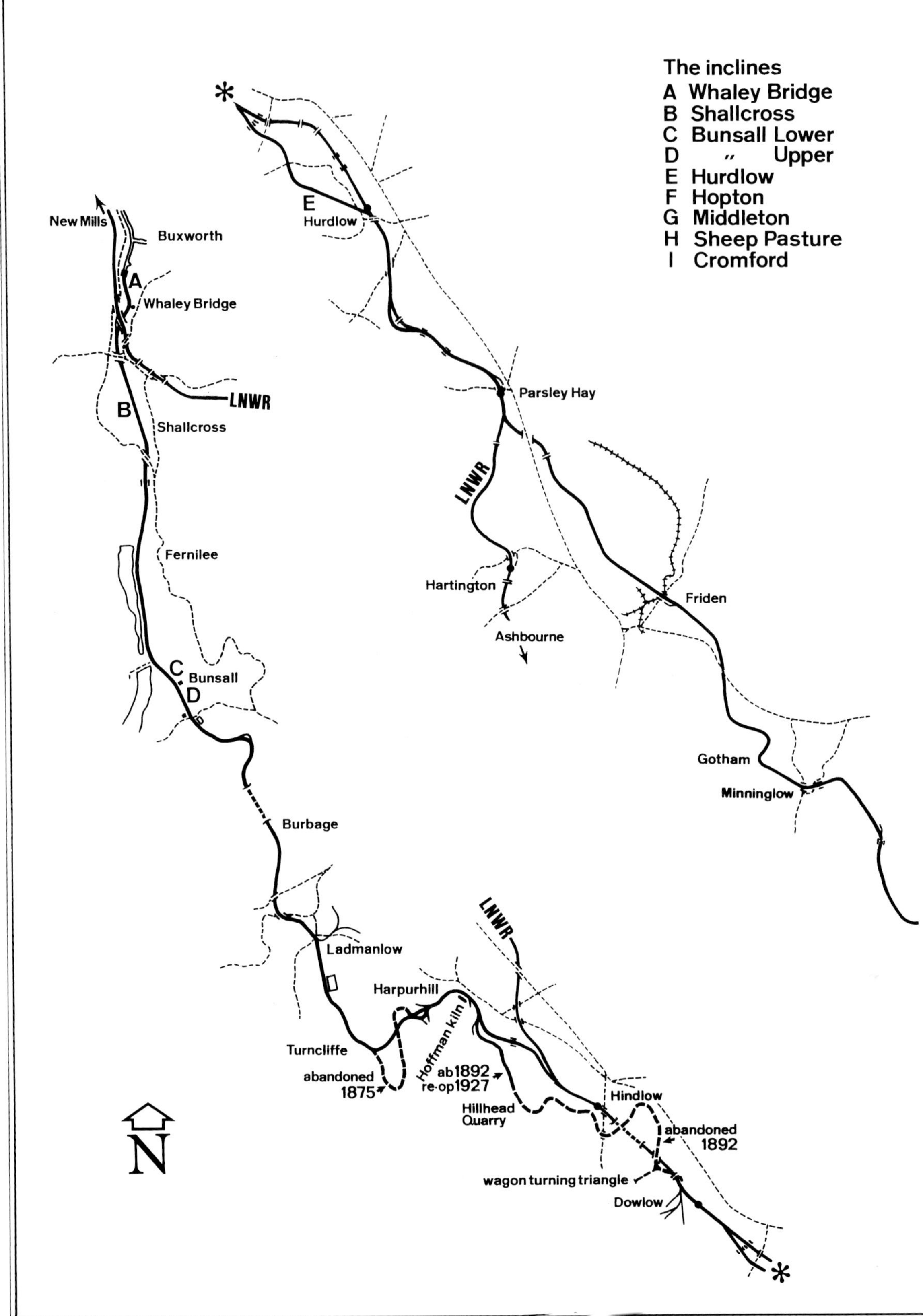
The inclines
A Whaley Bridge
B Shallcross
C Bunsall Lower
D " Upper
E Hurdlow
F Hopton
G Middleton
H Sheep Pasture
I Cromford
New Mills
Buxworth
A
Whaley Bridge
LNWR
B
Shallcross
Fernilee
C
Bunsall
D
Burbage
Ladmanlow
Harpurhill
Turncliffe
abandoned
1875
Hoffman kiln
ab1892
re-op1927
Hillhead
Quarry
Hindlow
abandoned
1892
wagon turning triangle
Dowlow
LNWR
E
Hurdlow
Parsley Hay
LNWR
Hartington
Ashbourne
Friden
Gotham
Minninglow
N

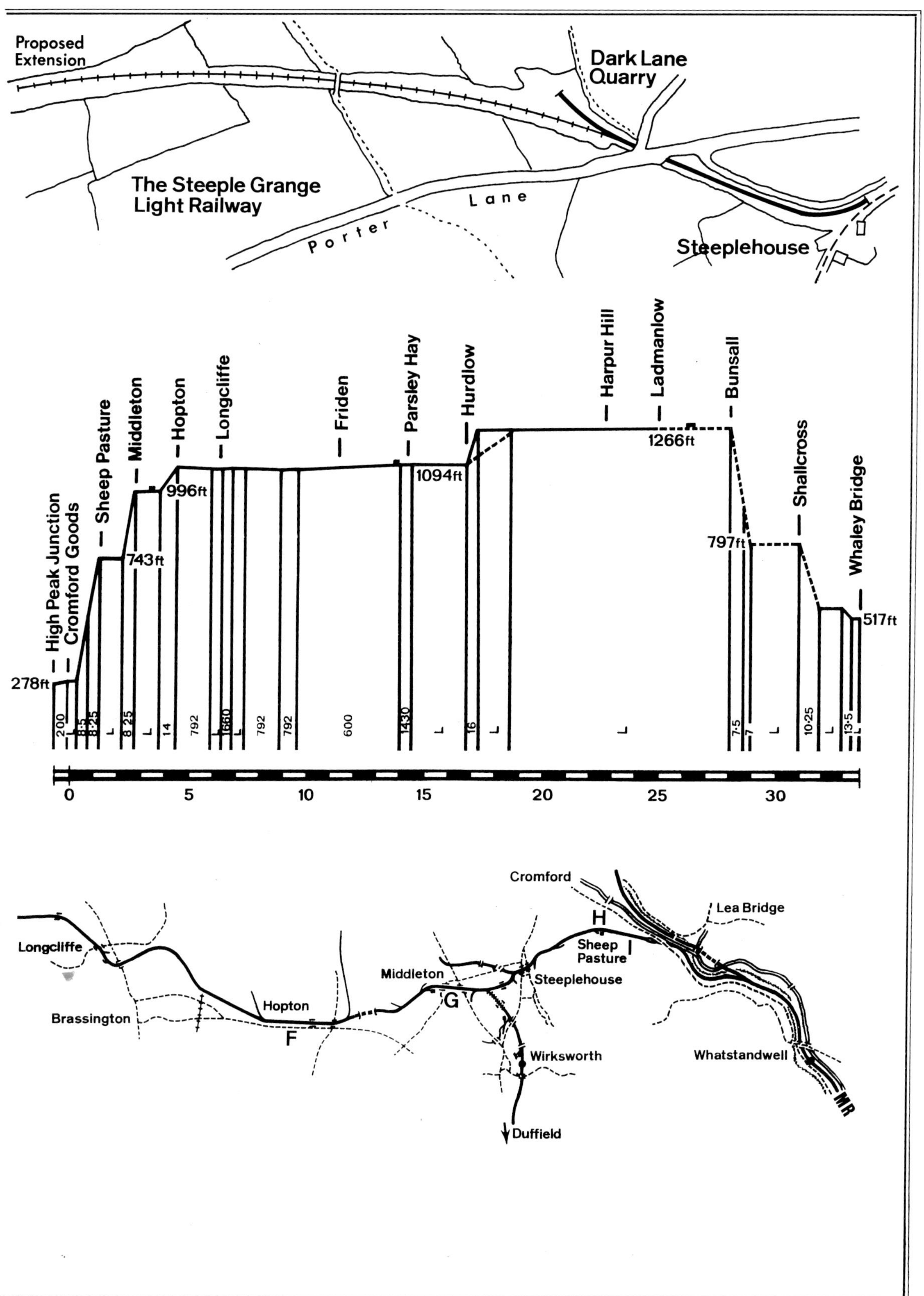
Proposed Extension
Dark Lane Quarry
The Steeple Grange Light Railway
Porter Lane
Steeplehouse
High Peak Junction
Cromford Goods
Sheep Pasture
Middleton
Hopton
Longcliffe
Friden
Parsley Hay
Hurdlow
Harpur Hill
Ladmanlow
Bunsall
Shallcross
Whaley Bridge
278ft
743ft
996ft
1094ft
1266ft
797ft
517ft
0
5
10
15
20
25
30
Cromford
Lea Bridge
H
Sheep Pasture
Longcliffe
Middleton
Steeplehouse
Brassington
Hopton
G
F
Wirksworth
Whatstandwell
MR
Duffield

condensing engine. He seemed unaware that Section 132 of the CHPR Act ruled that the company was 'not to draw water from feeders to the Peak Forest Canal'. The engine was erected and appears to have been at work by 1834. A William Brocklehurst, born 17 February 1835, was 'engine tenter' (engine tender, minder or operator) at Whaley Bridge from April 1856 to February 1860 when he was transferred to the Shallcross engine. The term 'tenter' was common in the 1830s to 1850s.

On 20 January 1836 Leonard wrote to James Meadows at Manchester:

'I should feel much obliged if you have an opportunity, and if it is not giving you too much trouble, if you would ascertain from someone on the Liverpool & Manchester Railway how long a rope lasts on the inclined planes through the tunnels at the Liverpool end before a new one becomes necessary and if such additional information as the size, price, weight, or tons drawn up in a given time, is easily attainable, all or any would be very acceptable, and to me very interesting. The subject has been discussed in committee with reference to our own inclined planes and I have received directions to ascertain as far as practicable the comparative cost weight and durability of ropes and chains and lay such information before the committee at their next meeting.

I trust the damage you sustained by the waggons running down the Whaley Inclined Plane is or will shortly be explained. I found we could do no good in attempting to repair the weighing machine and therefore concluded to send it to the makers as being the speediest and most efficient way of having it done'.

As early as the late 1830s cast iron rails were being replaced by wrought iron on wooden sleepers which left a quantity of stone blocks to be disposed of. On 26 March 1838 Leonard wrote to William Jessop Jr at Butterley Hall:

'I have seen Mr Arkwright and communicated to him the offer you have made for the old blocks. He considers the price a very low one and much below their value as wall stones, and thinks that at least they ought to be fetched from the place where they lie instead of being delivered at the canal at the place named in your letter.

The cost of loading them into waggons and unloading them at the canal wharf would be about 3d per ton. Instead of you fetching them where they lie it would be better if we delivered them at the canal wharf at 9d per ton.'

Replacement of the old cast-iron rails was spread over many years. On 7 March 1844 Leonard was directed to exchange old materials for new wrought-iron rails instead of selling them as had been done.

The high limestone-faced embankments on the Minninglow Farm land known as the 8-mile and 9-mile embankments needed extra support. On 12 April 1839 Leonard wrote to William Brittlebank, the solicitor at Winster, stating that for the 8-mile embankment 18 sq yd was wanted on the west side and possibly 10 sq yd on the east. For the 9-mile embankment 112 sq yd was wanted on the north side and up to 215 sq yd on the south.

On 26 January 1842 it was recorded that James Meadows had repeated a suggestion that the CHPR should build a warehouse at Whaley for the accommodation of the flour trade. No record has been found of this being done.

One of the unsolved mysteries of the CHPR was 'Middle Peak Incline'. Middle Peak quarry, above Wirksworth, was served by a branch from the foot of Middleton Incline. On 10 February 1842 an order was placed with Falconer Peach of Union Foundry, Derby, for 'pulley stops', two for each pulley, and on 9 September another for more pulleys, all for 'Middle Peak Incline'. On 11 October Wheatcroft was charged £48 5 10 'for work done on Middle Peak Incline'. There is no reference in the minutes to any method of haulage, that is if it were a separate incline. Could the name have been used to mean the Middleton incline?

The question of traffic on Sundays came up on 3 February 1842 when it was ordered that London traffic should be carried on Sundays 'subject to such regulations and times as Mr Leonard may consider necessary and so as to be as little objectionable as possible'.

John Leonard appears to have had some connection with the Cromford Canal although this was owned by a completely separate company. The canal was a unique piece of engineering in that its summit level extended 11¼ miles from its terminus at Cromford, over the great Wigwell aqueduct over the Derwent, through two short tunnels, across the Bullbridge aqueduct over the Amber (and later the North Midland Railway), through another short tunnel and the 3,063yd (formerly 2,966yd) Butterley tunnel to its junction with the Pinxton branch canal in the Erewash valley. From its opening in 1794 it was supplied by two feeders at the Cromford end. To supplement these a large beam pumping engine was installed at Leawood near Cromford to pump water from the Derwent into the canal. It was built by Graham & Co, Milton Ironworks, near Barnsley.

On 16 February 1845 Leonard wrote to Graham & Co:

'I think it not unlikely that a rather different arrangement of the building for the engine than the one which you have sent will be adopted and perhaps an entire house instead of a half one; if so it may possibly interfere in some degree with the boiler which had therefore better not be proceeded with for a few days until I have seen Mr Paterson (manager of the canal company)'.

Three days later he wrote again criticising the design of the Cornish boiler, 22ft long, 9ft diameter, with two flues and no return flue, and both direct to the chimney. He said the flues should unite and pass along a side flue and from there to the chimney. Also the boiler was too small for an engine of that size; it would require forcing to produce enough. The heating surface of 198ft^2 would give 2½ft^2 of heating surface per horse power whereas 5ft^2 was usual. He proposed a boiler about 35ft long, 7ft to 7ft 6in diameter, with two flues of such a size as would leave a wide space on each side, the flues uniting at the further end and returning by side flues as before in the usual way of Cornish boilers. He went on:

I suppose the boiler will be made of 3/8 in plate throughout. The plan you send appears to have a channel of masonry for conveying the water from the engine to the canal. You may possibly have omitted to notice that pipes were named in the agreement. The canal company have a meeting on the 26the inst when the site will probably be finally decided upon.

The boiler plates were ordered from the Butterley Co; on 22 April Leonard wrote to say that they were ordered some time ago and to ask for speedy delivery. On the 29th he wrote to Graham & Co:

Mr. Paterson agrees that there is no objection to your adapting two boilers instead of one in accordance with Mr Darlington's advice, if you think it proper to do so, especially as the two together exceed the dimensions to which I thought the single boiler ought to be limited. I prefer two flues through each boiler instead of one, each about 27in diameter.,

The pumping engine began operation in 1849. In 1979 the engine was restored to full working order by the Cromford Canal Society and it can often be seen working during summer week ends.

Certain regulations laid down in the CHPR Act of 1825 seem to have been overlooked from time to time. Section 110, on limiting weights, states: 'No wagon on four wheels to carry over 6 tons gross; six wheels 9 tons'. In fact six-wheeled wagons could not be used on the inclines because of possible derailment at the top where the wagon could be balanced on its middle wheels. On 6 May 1845 Leonard wrote to H. Heathcote, Blackwell near Bakewell:

'We cannot in future allow any more stones along the railway, or to be lifted by the crane, as heavy as the last large one you sent, 12 tons. I should be sorry not to afford you every accommodation in my power, but to deal in such weights we are running the risk of serious accident'.

In a letter to Wheatcroft & Son, Buckland Hollow near Belper, he wrote on 14 May 1845: 'I believe the Committee of the High Peak Railway will be disposed to reduce their tonnage rates to the same extent as the Canal Company's and their plane dues from 1½d to 1d per ton each, viz Tonnage 33 miles at ½d, 1s 4½d. Inclined Planes 9 at 1d, 9d. Total 2s 1½d per ton'.

At a meeting of the agents of the Cromford, Peak Forest and Ashton Canal Companies and the CHPR on 7 July 1845 to consider reducing the tonnage rates on the London – Manchester through traffic to meet competition, it was decided that a reduction of ½d/ton/mile was absolutely necessary to secure that branch of the traffic but, in consequence of the expense of working the inclined planes of the CHPR, the railway must charge, in addition to ½d/ton/mile, 4½d/ton/mile to meet the cost of operating the inclines. Considering that the actual cost of working the inclines was over 1s 0d per ton, the meeting agreed that the proposed rate of 1s 9d to be taken by the railway would not be sufficiently remunerative as only 9d would remain on 33 miles of railway. Therefore the committee did not feel able to reduce the rate more than from 2s 8d now charged, to 2s 0d. This decision was communicated to Wheatcroft & Son in a letter on 8 July 1845.

The financial affairs of the CHPR Co were shaky from the start. Of the £164,400 authorized by the Act of 1825 the shareholders subscribed £127,700 in shares of £100, and £31,910 was raised by mortgage. The holder of the largest number of shares, 200, was John Wright of Lenton, Nottingham, a banker and a partner in the Butterley Company. Two, A.M. Anson and Henry Digby, held 100, and three, Edward Lloyd, S.R. Brooks and Charles Buchanan held 50.

A balance sheet dated 9 June 1841 signed by the chairman Peter Arkwright and presented at the 'General Annual Meeting of the Proprietors' of the CHPR at the Greyhound Inn, Cromford, on 10 June showed an income of £5,040 against an expenditure of £5,715. The heaviest burden was interest on mortgages to 25 March 1833, £2,393. Operating expenses, £2,020 included wages for 'engine tenders', £626; coal for engines, £439; wages for repairs to engines and machinery £301; materials for these repairs £493. Tonnages for the year ended 22 May 1841 compared with 1840 were:

	tons	£	Increase (+) Decrease (-)	
Limestone and lime	29,924	656	+4,723	+£63
Coal and coke	16,810	1,358	+150	+£7
Corn, malt, flour etc	6,992	1,035	+307	+£50
Packages	6,298	1,210	+454	+£102
Minerals	2,040	212	-1,195	-£118
Timber	1,180	200	-23	
Iron, lead, etc	756	143	+137	+£27
Building stone, etc	266	18	-120	-£7
Miscellaneous	138	6		-£5

Looking back at Jessop's forecasts of traffic in his report of 1824, tonnage of corn, malt and flour was well short of his forecast of 60,000 tons. Tonnage of limestone and lime, however, was above Jessop's forecast of 10,000 tons.

A second Act had to be obtained in 1843[2] to obtain powers to raise by mortgage a further £54,800 of which £22,890 was used to discharge part of the floating debt of £46,915 which, at 31 August 1842 was still owed to the Butterley Company for stationary engines, machinery, rails and other ironwork. This left a second floating debt of £24,025. The future of the CHPR Co looked grim.

NOTES

1 CHPR Letter Book PRO RAIL 144/1
2 CHPR Act 9 May 1843 c 18

3. The end of isolation

In the ten years following the opening of the CHPR railways were opened all over England and the CHPR was becoming aware of its isolation. The North Midland Railway, Derby to Leeds, opened from Derby to Masborough on 11 May 1840. At Ambergate, where it left the Derwent valley, it was only 4½ miles from the Cromford terminus of the CHPR. George Stephenson, engineer of the NMR, proposed a connection to the CHPR and a plan, dated February 1840, was prepared by Frederick Swanwick (1810-85), George Stephenson's principal assistant, and Charles P. Ireland[1]. It shows the intended railway running from the wharf by the Cromford Canal along the course of the junction railway of 1853 and the route of the Matlock Railway (see below) to join the NMR east of Ambergate. On 7 March 1842 the proposal was discussed at a meeting of the CHPR management at Whatstandwell[2]. No application had been made to Parliament. A further plan was prepared[3] showing an identical extension with branches near Ambergate to Morley Park Ironworks including an incline up at 1 in 8 on Morley Park Branch No. 2. Another meeting on 1 December 1842, chaired by Captain Goodwin, was attended by William Jessop Jr, Charles Hurt, Robert Arkwright, Robert Stephenson, Mr Mold, Andrew Brittlebank and John Leonard. Nothing was decided but Stephenson said he would communicate with Mr Brittlebank on the subject.

The scheme was soon overtaken by the pace of railway development. To understand the history of the CHPR from the mid 1840s it is necessary to digress. In an attempt to gain access to Manchester, the Midland Railway (into which the North Midland had been amalgamated in 1844) sought the support of the Manchester & Birmingham Railway and together they promoted the Manchester, Buxton, Matlock & Midlands Junction Railway to connect the North Midland line at Ambergate with the Manchester & Birmingham at Cheadle near Stockport, 42 miles. This railway was promoted in conjunction with the Ambergate, Nottingham & Boston & Eastern Junction Railway to form a route from Manchester to the eastern Midlands round the south of the Pennines.

Meanwhile, in November 1845, the Cromford Canal Co proposed the sale of its undertaking to the MBM&MJ (to be referred to henceforth as the Matlock Railway). This did not please the management of the CHPR and at a meeting at Cromford on 9 May 1846 John Leonard ordered that a deputation consisting of Messrs Hurt, Goodwin and Jessop should go to London to assist in opposing the sale. The opposition did not succeed. Powers for the purchase of the Cromford Canal were given to the Matlock Co by the Cromford Canal Sale Act of 1846, and powers to complete the purchase in the canal company's Act of 1851[4]. Under the Matlock company's Act of 1852[5] the purchase, for £103,500, was completed on 30 August. In March 1846 the undertaking of the Peak Forest Canal Co was absorbed by the Sheffield Ashton & Manchester Railway[6] at the same time as that company became the Manchester, Sheffield & Lincolnshire Railway[7].

The Matlock and the Ambergate, Nottingham etc railway bills received the Royal Assent on 16 July 1846[8]. The Matlock Railway soon found itself in difficulties. The Railway Mania had collapsed and capital was not forthcoming, and whichever route was taken beyond Rowsley, up the Derwent or Wye valleys, would involve massive and expensive engineering works. Also, on the same date, 16 July, the London & North Western Railway was formed, with the Manchester & Birmingham as a constituent[9]. As a competing route to Manchester the Matlock Railway no longer had the support of the Manchester & Birmingham. The result of these difficulties was that all that came to be built was the 11½ mile section from Ambergate to Rowsley, opened on 4 June 1849.

A notice issued by the Railway Office, Cromford, printed on 20 January 1847 announced a proposal by the proprietors of the CHPR

'to farm or lease, for one, two or three years from 25 March next, on the following conditions:– the Rates Tolls and Duties arising therefrom. The Lessee will be required to keep open the railway for public traffic, by the proper working of the Steam Engines, and Inclined-planes; and will be subject to the payment of all rates, taxes, and rents, and to the observance of the provisions of the Act of Parliament, for making and maintaining the said Railway, and the rules, byelaws, orders, and regulations of the Company.

And the Company further propose to enter into a Contract with the Lessee, for maintaining and keeping in complete repair during the continuance of the Lease, the Railway, the Houses, buildings, wharfs, warehouses, cranes, embankments, and, excavations, and all bridges, Tunnels, culverts, draines, (sic) fences, reservoirs, Stationary Engines, machinery, chains, pulleys, apparatus, and all other works thereon or connected therewith, so that on the termination of the lease, the Railway in all respects, and all the buildings, machinery and works thereof, shall be in as perfect and good a state as when entered upon, otherwise full compensation will be required for any deterioration or deficiency.

Tenders to be sent to Mr. Leonard, Railway Office, near Cromford, and to state a separate sum for the Rent of the Rates, Tolls and Duties, subject to the working of Engines Planes &c. And another sum for maintaining and keeping in perfect repair the Railway and all other works &c, as before proposed.

Good and sufficient security will be required for payment of the Rent, and for the due and effectual performance of the other stipulations.'

These were totally unacceptable demands and, as might be expected, no tenders were received or, if they were, none was accepted.

Perhaps this was Leonard's final fling, for from

1865 cast-iron bridge on Middleton incline, GR 279552, 9 July 1973 *(John Marshall)*

Newhaven tunnel from south, July 1941 *(John Marshall)*

Below left Plaque at south end of Newhaven tunnel, 29 March 1984 *(John Marshall)*

Below right Plaque on north end of Newhaven tunnel, 18 March 1973 *(John Marshall)*

about this time, after directing the affairs of the CHPR since its opening, he disappeared from the records and no further information about him has been found. There is nothing in the minutes to explain the circumstances in which he left the CHPR or what happened to him. The duties of secretary were taken over by Francis Barton, and for the time being there appeared to be no engineer in charge. Some idea of Barton's style of letter writing can be gained from the following example, dated 31 May 1849, addressed to Messrs Peach & Son[10].

'Will thanks you to send us 2 pistons for 20 Horse engine you have the pattern. Also 2 rings the same as those supplied last week but from a larger pattern. Those you sent were wrong being cast from a smaller pattern the diameter of the rings now wanted is somewhere about 26 inches outside'

As a through route the CHPR was in competition with canals. The following letter from the Butterley Co is dated 16 July 1849 and signed by George Staley:

'We have about 700 tons of bridge works to send to Liverpool and we beg to ask if the CHPR Co will make any reduction in their rate of tonnage if we sent it over their line. From enquiries we have made we find our cheapest route is by way of the Grand Trunk Canal to Runcorn and unless your company is disposed to make some reduction for so large a quantity we shall, we fear, have to take that route'.

Staley wrote again a week later because he had had no reply. At last, on 7 September, Barton wrote to him:

'I have placed our correspondence on the subject of a reduction of tonnage on the bridge works before our committee and am directed to state that in the absence of any information being supplied by you to justify the reduction they are at a loss to know on what ground you apply for it.

Staley wrote an exasperated reply saying that the reasons had already been stated. The bridge works were sent by canal. Another letter to Staley at Butterley, dated 20 November 1850, reminds him that the CHPR Co is not itself a carrier. Barton mentioned that there were objections to himself being a trader on the line. Messrs Wheatcroft & Son or Nathaniel Wheatcroft Jr would undertake the carrying or, if he preferred, Staley could hire CHPR wagons.

To return to the Matlock Railway, it passed only a short distance from the Cromford wharf of the CHPR. Soon after its opening the question of a junction was being discussed. Arguments followed concerning the responsibility for the cost of the junction line. The CHPR agreed to build it at its expense and asked the Matlock Co only for permission to have a siding at the junction.

At a meeting at the Midland Hotel, Derby, on 19 January 1851 the directors of the Matcock Co informed the CHPR that, because of their agreement with the LNWR and Midland companies, they were unable to give a definite answer concerning the junction and suggested that a memorial should be drawn up and sent to the directors of the two companies.

Agreement was reached on 19 January 1852, but by then the Matlock Co had agreed to lease its line to the LNWR and Midland. The joint lease, for 19 years from 1 July 1852, must be one of the strangest alliances in railway history: the Midland was in it for the purpose of reaching Manchester and the LNWR for the purpose of preventing the Midland from reaching Manchester.

With no authorizing Act the CHPR Co went ahead with a plan and specification for the junction line and on 6 October the following advertisement for tenders appeared in the *Derby Mercury.*

CROMFORD AND HIGH PEAK RAILWAY.
TO CONTRACTORS.

THE COMMITTEE of MANAGEMENT of the CROMFORD and HIGH PEAK RAILWAY, are prepared to receive TENDERS for the execution of a BRANCH LINE from the Manchester, Buxton, Matlock, and Midlands Junction Railway, to the terminus of the Comford and High Peak Railway, near Cromford, a distance of 58 Chains.

Plans and Specification may be seen at the Company's Offices, near Cromford, from THURSDAY, the 7th; and sealed Tenders addressed to the Committee, must be delivered at the above Offices, not later than FRIDAY, the 15th October instant.

The Committee will meet at the GREYHOUND INN, Cromford, on SATARDAY, the 16th instant, at Eleven o'clock in the Forenoon, to LET the WORK, when Parties Tendering must attend.

By order,
FRANCIS BARTON, Agent.
Railway Office, Cromford, 4th Oct., 1852.

No record of the name of the contractor or the price of the contract has been found. Four weeks later the following paragraph was printed in the same paper:

CROMFORD AND HIGH PEAK RAILWAY. – Our readers are aware, that an advertisement has appeared in this paper, for tenders for forming a junction between this line and the Midlands, (sic) at or near Cromford; the contract for which work has been taken. The necessity for it has arisen, through the value of the well-known stone called Hopton-Wood stone (a kind of marble, obtained from a quarry in the neighbourhood of Wirksworth), having lately increased in consequence of its use in a new method about to be employed for fluxing iron, in the Potteries. A company has been formed, who have laid a line of rails from the High Peak Railway to the Quarry, and we believe, as soon as the junction is formed with the Rowsley and Ambergate branch of the Midland Railway, the loose blocks of stone, together with the rubble and rubbish, will be sent down the line to the extent of many thousands of tons in the year, and will materially increase the traffic on this line. We are glad to see this improvement in the neighbourhood of Wirksworth, and hope it may lead to other and greater benefits. There will necessarily be a great number of hands required, not only in forming the line, but permanently.

The junction line was built on a shelf above the

Derwent to join the Matlock line at High Peak Junction just south of Leawood tunnel. It was opened on 21 February 1853. There was no authorizing Act, but its construction and opening were confirmed in Section 6 of the CHPR Act of 1855[11] to be mentioned later. So, after more than 20 years of isolation, the CHPR was at last connected to the expanding national railway network.

Locomotive Foreman Merrill and Traffic Inspector Jack Smith by the signal at Cromford Wharf level crossing

An interesting article on the passenger service appeared in the *Derby Mercury* on 20 September 1854:

A SPLENDID TRIP FOR THIS HOT WEATHER (FROM A CORRESPONDENT)

A short time ago, we understood that the proprietors of the "High Peak Railway" had determined to put a passenger train on their line. Having known the line for twenty-five years, and gone over it and crossed it in all directions, we made up our minds to have a trip over it under the new circumstances, and consequently joined it at Steeple Houses, near Wirksworth, on one of those very hot days more than a week ago. The carriage (only one) we found admirably, but plainly fitted up for the comfort of passengers, both outside and in – the inside will accommodate about sixteen, and the out, fourteen – thus carrying in all thirty passengers, and this drawn by one horse over all the levels, and changed, of course, at certain stations. Away we went at a good sharp trot, and the motion we found to be exceedingly pleasant. The third, or Middleton incline, we soon reached; two had been ascended from the terminus, two miles below. On these inclines, eight in number, the great difficulty was at first felt as to what the public might think of them as dangerous or not; but, by adding two powerful breaks to the carriage, all danger is avoided, for the conductor told us he could stop the carriage on the steepest part of these inclines, by his breaks, in about one minute – consequently, no one could feel the slightest fear. Here, at the bottom of the incline, the horse was removed and sent upwards, while the carriage was attached to the chain of the stationary engine, seen pouring out its volumes of smoke at the top. Presently we heard the clanging of the massive chain over its multitude of fixed pullies or wheels, to steady its motion, and away we went at a very respectable and regular pace, and soon reached the top, passing through heavy cuttings of the first limestone. But what a commanding view we had here! Behind us we had the pine-topped Barrel Edge and Black Rocks. Onward, sweeping eastward, appeared Riber Hill, Lea Woods, with their fine terrace roadway, at the end of which towered loftily Crich Cliff and Stand; beyond this, Crich Chase and the rich and fertile coal districts appeared. On the south, the view was extensive and beautiful – for it overlooked the greater part of the fine agricultural district of South Derbyshire, even far beyond the glorious Trent River. The little old mining town of Wirksworth appeared almost beneath our feet. Time will not permit us to enter into details, nor is it needful. We now reached the second plain – our horse was attached, and on we went, passing through a short tunnel, midway between the Middleton and Hopton inclines, which we soon reached, and arrived in perfect safety at the Hopton Station, the highest point on the southern part of the line. The view here, though extensive, is not so varied or fine as the one we had just left. But now came into view the noble Thorp Cloud at the southern end of Dove Dale, as well as the great heights connected with the Weaver Hills, stretching far into Staffordshire. Another fine range, running northward, bounded the lovely Dove Dale. Here we arrived at the end of the twelve-mile level. The line at this point tends to the north. Passing over Brassington Moor and Pastures, we crossed over the road leading to Dove Dale. From hence the view was very remarkable, as well as beautiful; for beneath us, to the west, lay the rugged and bold features of what has not been inaptly termed the "Trossachs of Derbyshire". Vast numbers of jutting and pinnacled rocks, some rising in bold groups, others in single masses, adorned with brushwood, creeping plants, and miniature pine plantations, with the beautiful green glades, sloping among and between them, and stretching far down into the valley below, present to the eye a rich and striking picture, where the rude and the beautiful seem to combine and sweetly harmonize together. We soon reached the station of Parsley Hay, not far from Hartington, and very soon also reached Hurdlow, at the foot of the last and longest incline. This is not near so steep as the others, and we should think a locomotive engine would run up as easily as on the Gloucester and Birmingham line; – be that as it may, here also is a stationary engine which hauled us up very nicely, and then we reached the summit level of this remarkable railway, which has been constructed now more than thirty years, at a cost of 300,000 l., forming (when first constructed), a most important connection between the great grain counties east and south, and the equally important mining and manufacturing districts to the north. The hundreds of thousands of loads of wheat and flour, besides all kinds of merchandise, which passed over it some years ago was really astonishing; now, since the midland and other connecting lines opened, it has reduced the traffic to almost a mere local one. The proprietors do right, therefore, in making it a passenger line, which cannot fail to prove a convenience to all parties within its range, and we hope, too, pay the proprietors well.

From our splendid position on the summit level, we could command an immense view to almost every point of the wide horizon, our altitude being upwards of 1,000 feet above the sea.

The frowning dark ridges of the gritstone moors to the north, seen stretching eastward as far as Castleton, and being also nearly in the midst of the loftiest of the undulating limestone hills, the effect was very grand and imposing. The top of this incline commences the second twelve-mile level. Upon this, as on the one we had passed over, a small engine plied constantly at one time, but only to do the company's own business. These are dispensed with and sold; but one, which was bought by Mr. Gisborne, still plies between his large lime pits and the top of the great incline in the Goyte valley. We soon passed these kilns, and then Buxton came into view, with its fine Crescent, well-built stone houses, and beautiful church; and, as it is now laid out and adorned with exquisite ornate pleasure-garden work of every kind, with splendid taste, in the full blaze of a noonday sun it looked magnificent:– and the effect was heightened by its surrounding framework, which is composed of bleak and sterile hills and healthy moors, that administer the healthy and balmy breeze to the visitors of this charming watering place. The line takes a curve to avoid the deep valley of Buxton; but we soon reached the Ladmanlow station a mile to the west of it, and situated at the foot of Axe Edge.

We have already exceeded our limits, and must conclude, merely stating that, some way from this station, we pass through a long tunnel, driven through the gritstone into the valley of the Goyte, which indeed is interesting and in parts beautiful. Through this valley we descended to Whaley, where we arrived at 12 o'clock – thus passing over thirty-two miles in four hours. This is a single line the greater part of its length, with proper sidings to let other trains pass.

Several interesting details are revealed in this article. It appears that the CHPR had taken over operation of the passenger service from Wheatcroft using a specially built vehicle. Second, it suggests that passengers actually rode up and down the inclines, though if it really took the guard up to a minute to operate the brake, on an incline of 1 in 8 or steeper, it is unlikely that 'no one could feel the slightest fear'. Third, it seems that CHPR locomotives did not work at that time on the summit level, though a privately-owned one did.

In the 1854 Bill the CHPR sought powers to purchase or to lease, and to work, the Harpur Hill Lime Works. The Chairman of the House of Lords Committee, however, objected to railway companies embarking in any undertakings other than that for which they were incorporated, and the powers were refused. In his report to the directors at the first meeting of the CHPR after its re-incorporation, held at Derby on 8 August 1855, the chairman stated that arrangements had been made with Harpur Hill Lime Works for the CHPR to secure all the traffic, and that the company would be better without the risk as lime burners.

The position of chief engineer had remained vacant since John Underwood left in 1847-8. In 1854 the company made what was to prove an unwise decision to appoint Captain William Scarth Moorsom (1804-63). Moorsom was an engineer of questionable merit, best remembered as engineer of the Birmingham & Gloucester Railway completed in 1841. With its notorious Lickey incline and its poor connections with Droitwich, Worcester, Tewkesbury, Cheltenham and even Gloucester, it hardly ranks as one of Britains best main lines. Moorsom was to prove an additional financial burden on the already overstretched CHPR. With unbridled enthusiasm he produced schemes with little apparent consideration of how the money was to be provided.

In 1854 the Stockport, Disley & Whaley Bridge Railway received its Act, with strong LNWR support[12]. In the same year the CHPR sought powers for a deviation line from the north end of Buxton tunnel, crossing a viaduct 136ft high and falling on a uniform gradient of 1 in 40, avoiding the Bunsall and Shallcross inclines and joining the SD & WB at its terminus at Whaley Bridge. The plan and section were prepared by Captain Moorsom.

The deviation line was strongly and successfully opposed by the Manchester, Sheffield & Lincolnshire Railway which was then planning a line of its own to Buxton, and it had to be withdrawn from the CHPR Bill. The connection to the SD & WB was retained but this was constructed under Sections 3-5 of the SD & WB Act of 1855[13]. Section 12 of the Act ruled that the SD & WB should not be opened until the junction railway was completed and ready for traffic. Power was given to the LNWR to subscribe and to become shareholders to the extent of £85,000 and the CHPR was to contribute £3,750 and was to be allowed to appoint a director.

The CHPR Act 1855[11] repealed the Acts of 1825 and 1843 and re-incorporated the company, and defined its route as extending from the Peak Forest Canal to a junction with the Manchester, Buxton, Matlock & Midlands Junction Railway. It authorized the raising of a further £20,000 capital and up to £6,000 on mortgage. Section 54 gave powers to construct a connecting line from the top of the Whaley Bridge incline to a junction with the SD & WBR at the back of the Jodrell Arms Inn in the parish of Taxal although, as already mentioned, this was built under the SD & WB Act. Sections 68-71 concerned carriage of passengers and Section 77 ruled that the railway was to be subject to BOT inspection before passengers were carried.

The first ordinary meeting of the proprietors under the new Act was held at the Midland Hotel, Derby, on 8 August 1855. At this meeting Francis Barton was officially appointed as secretary, a post he had occupied on a temporary basis since Underwood left.

In his report to the CHPR directors presented at the meeting on 8 August 1855[14] Moorsom recommended alterations at Buxton (Ladmanlow) estimated to cost £2,800. About 60 curves required alteration; 18 had been pegged out on the ground. The estimated cost was £4,788 including £513 for 8½ acres of land and £288 for engineering. Another 16 were estimated at £2,588. A third batch, of 26, were small and would cost about £30 each, but even these amounted to £780. The total for 60 curves was £8,146.

Alterations to earthworks and permanent way on the Cromford and Bunsall inclines were estimated to cost £5,700. Conversion of these inclines for operation with one engine at the head of each (the only sound and practicable proposal made by Moorsom) was estimated at £2,400. A further £3,800 was expected to be required for two locomotives and tenders but he had been offered two for £2,000. There was no indication of how he thought all this money was to be found.

Plans and specification for alteration of the line at the foot of Bunsall incline were submitted by Moorsom on 8 November 1855. A contract (price not given) for this work was let to George Farnsworth who also had a contract for alterations to the embankment at the top of Bunsall incline, but he lost this when, as he claimed, the work was placed in other hands. On 5 November 1856 he requested compensation of £123 6s 8d. Barton was requested to write to Moorsom explaining that the work was not proceeded with and therefore was not in other hands.

Moorsom reported on 30 January 1856 that the stationary engines were 'much out of repair'. Also many parts of Buxton tunnel were defective. Work had begun on converting the Cromford and Bunsall inclines to be worked by a single engine each. When the alterations were completed the inclines would be worked by wire ropes. Dispensing with the two stationary engines was expected to save nearly £600 a year. The work involved modifying the gradient in the middle where the wagons were transferred from one chain to the other.

A report to the CHPR directors on 27 February 1856 listed the rolling stock as:

Common wagons without springs, for coal	82
Harper (sic) Hill lime wagons	45
Goods spring wagons	14
Coal spring wagons for Whaley	4
Trucks	2
Under repairs	7
New sample truck	1
Passenger carriage	1
	156
Canal boats for coal	8
Canal boats for goods	1
Horses	20

Limestone traffic was increasing steadily during this period. Rates for coal from Cromford to Ladmanlow were reduced in October 1855 from 2s 3d to 1s 6d per ton. On 5 November 1856 Robert Broome was requested to purchase 15 wagons at £15 each 'or any less number'.

The solicitor of the company, William Brittlebank lived at Oddo near Winster and had his office in Wirksworth. He resigned in October 1855 and his place was taken by Philip Hubbersty, also at Wirksworth, and Andrew Brittlebank of Winster. In 1856 the company decided it could no longer afford to retain Captain Moorsom as engineer. On 30 April 1857 William Smith was engaged as secretary and engineer at £150 per annum. Smith, born in 1825, was trained at Preston where, in 1840, he was articled to J.J. Myres. His appointment to the CHPR followed a period of varied engineering experience.

At a meeting on 31 December 1856 Mr William Needham was appointed managing director of the company at £250 per annum. William Jessop retired from the board and Robert Broome of Whaley Bridge was elected a director in place of Jessop, but on 26 February 1857 when George Strutt resigned as a director William Jessop was reappointed in his place. At a special directors' meeting at Derby on 11 April Robert Broome was appointed managing director and general superintendent with power to appoint and dismiss subordinates 'as he may think proper'.

It was agreed at the meeting on 29 October 1857 that parliamentary powers should be sought to raise further capital and to lease or sell the line to the London & North Western; Midland; Stockport, Disley & Whaley Bridge or Manchester, Sheffield & Lincolnshire Railway.

The Buxton Lime Co opened a branch to the Grin lime kilns near Ladmanlow early in 1857. As mentioned in connection with the Cromford junction line, a quarry was opened at Hopton Wood in the early 1850s by David Wheatcroft, and a

J94 0-6-0 saddle tank 68034 at High Peak Junction with SLS/MLS special on 22 April 1961

steeply-graded branch was built down to it from near the foot of Hopton incline. To haul wagons up from the quarry David Wheatcroft was given permission, on 31 July 1856, to erect a stationary engine beside the CHPR on the opposite side to the branch and to carry a cable underneath the line. The engine was powered by a wagon-type boiler, the remains of which can still be seen. The Middle Peak quarry above Wirksworth was also being developed with a connection from the CHPR near the foot of Middleton incline.

In November 1856 William Wheatcroft started a quarry about half way down Middleton incline, and a siding connection was laid in. Obviously a siding could not be worked from a continuous chain incline, so to make it possible the incline was converted to single line and the Butterley Co was engaged to make the necessary alterations to the incline and the stationary engine. The chain was replaced by a hemp rope 800 yd long. The engine was rebuilt to work with a winding drum. Examination of the engine fails to reveal how this was carried out. An article in *The Engineer,* 22 November 1912 p552, stated that drawings of the Middleton engine dated 1865 were in the Mechanical Engineer's office at Crewe. These drawings, which should solve the mystery, cannot be found. They may no longer exist.

The single-line working gave considerable trouble. On 29 October 1857 the secretary drew the attention of the CHPR board to the insecure state of the incline as a result of Wheatcroft working his quarries in such a way as to risk breaking rails and damaging the rope, and interfering with the traffic. The quarries were apparently worked for only a few years, but troubles continued to beset the incline as was revealed in two letters from William Smith to William Cawkwell, general manager of the LNWR, on 8 and 15 June 1865. He explained an accident on 6 June, caused by breakage of the rope, when an old tender used as a water tank ran away and collided with two wagons belonging to the Hopton Lime Co. The trouble was caused by the rope running across the winding drum when winding up light loads. On lowering a heavy load the slack would suddenly be taken up causing a jerk on the rope and possible breakage. Smith added that the quarry had 'long ceased to be worked'. He urged restoration of balanced working at an estimated cost of £890, and outlined the economic advantages in facilitating the passing of traffic and reducing wear on the engine, but another 29 years were to pass before this was carried out. It seems extraordinary that this expensive alteration, causing such danger and inconvenience, should have been carried out in the first place for such a small quarry. Possibly it was this that brought about the dismissal of Moorsom as engineer.

The Butterley Co was awarded the contract for the alteration of the Cromford/Sheep Pasture inclines on 28 May 1857 for operation with an endless wire rope and to relay the incline with wrought-iron rails. Robert Broome was authorized to order a wire rope from Glass Elliott & Co. There is no mention in the minutes of the similar work on the Bunsall incline, but this came into operation as a single incline on 6 June 1857 and Sheep Pasture on 16 October. Although the company's minutes on 30 January 1856 recorded that on completion of the alterations the inclines would be worked by wire ropes, it appears that hemp ropes were installed. The first positive record of wire ropes was on Bunsall incline on 3 September 1862 and on Sheep Pasture on 19 February 1863. The last hemp rope was installed on Shallcross incline on 22 May 1865, and it was the last to be replaced by a wire rope, on 27 February 1868. From hand-written notes on rope changes, rope life seemed to vary enormously; hemp 1-3 years, iron 1-2 years, later steel wire 2-3 years.

It was reported on 30 July 1857 that the works between Whaley Bridge and Buxton had made steady progress and would be completed by the time the junction with the SD & WB was ready.

A loaded wagon about to be rolled forward to the 'hanging on' position at Sheep Pasture in 1949
(Frank D. Woodall)

Direct communication would then be made between the LNWR and the Midland and a great increase in traffic was expected. At the same time a notice was issued stating that the Hopton and Middle Peak quarries near Wirksworth had been taken and were about to be extensively worked by a company formed for that purpose.

A new book of rules, regulations and by-laws was submitted by the secretary on 25 March 1858. It was ordered to be printed and a proof copy sent to each director for comment. This was the first proper CHPR rule book and it replaced the sheets of rules, orders and regulations issued by Francis Barton on 3 March 1853[15]. The new rule book, dated 2 August 1858, was signed by William Smith and printed by Cave & Sever, Palatine Buildings, Hunts Bank, Manchester. Besides standard general rules applicable to all railways, it contained sections specifically related to the CHPR, such as inclined planes, Flymen and Slowmen. Flymen operated the through traffic and passenger carriage; slowmen the stopping freight traffic. Men working the inclines were 'planemen'.

The number of men employed on the railway increased from 72 in 1856 to 108 in 1860. In 1858 there were 10 platelayers, in 1860 18, a result of the extensive relaying work. Engine drivers increased from 10 to 13. Wages were low: in the 1830s labourers received less than 10s a week; a permanent way ganger 10s to 12s and a stationary engineman 18s. They had risen a few shillings by the 1860s. On 22 March 1866 Smith recommended raising the wages of George Hawley, carpenter at Cromford, from 21s to 22s a week, and on 14 June he brought to the attention of the LNWR Special Committee (by then the CHPR was part of the LNWR; see below) a memorial from platelayers on the 'High Peak Line' for an advance of wages. Gangers received 2s 6d a day and labourers 2s 4d. Smith was authorized to increase their pay by 1s a week 'should he find it necessary to do it'. On his recommendation it was ordered on 19 July that the wages of Henry Roper, engineer on the Bunsall incline, should be raised from 21s to 22s a week, and on 22 August the wages of George Goodson, locomotive driver, from 17s to 18s a week.

It was the wives who kept the homes going, making ladies' straw bonnets and other articles by hand. Yet some of the families managed to save enough money to buy fields, sometimes costing £800, in which they kept cows.

The 1855 Act gave the company powers to operate its own traffic, whereupon it took over the passenger service. The directors reported on 30 January 1856 that they did not intend to make much provision for passenger traffic until the SD & WB was opened, 'but as the carriage which ran between Cromford and Whaley last summer was a convenience to the district and some profit to the company they intend to put it on again'. From this it appears that it ran in summer only, and that it was operated by the railway company. A timetable published locally on 2 July 1856 (see illustrations) give details of a service between Cromford and Ladmanlow at a fare of 3s 6d inside and 2s 6d outside. So it appears that the coach with inside and outside accommodation continued to operate. How long the company ran the horse-drawn service is not known. The 1858 rule book forbade the carrying of passengers up and down the inclines. Rule 31 added: 'all passengers to be compelled to wait till the descending train is in motion before they proceed to walk down such inclined plane; and the ascending train not to be drawn up until all the passengers have arrived at the top'. By this date a brake van with passenger accommodation, known as a 'fly', was attached to the rear of a through goods train.

The SD & WB was opened on 9 June 1857, and on 17 August the connection to the CHPR was officially opened. But the bridge over the Goyt was not ready for locomotives, and wagons were hauled across by the contractor's horses.

Useful information is contained in a diary

CROMFORD AND HIGH PEAK RAILWAY

CHEAP TRAVELLING

FROM WIRKSWORTH TO BUXTON, FOR 2s. 6d.

A

PASSENGER CARRIAGE

HAS COMMENCED RUNNING BETWEEN

CROMFORD & BUXTON.

At eight o'clock every morning (Sundays excepted) arriving at

Steeple House for Wirksworth at 8 15; Middleton, 8 30; Hopton, 8 45; Longcliff, for Brassington and Winkter, 9 15, Friden, 9 45, Parsley Hay, for Hartington, 10 0; Hurdlow, 10 20; Hindlow, for Longnor 11 15; Ladmanlow, 12 0; with an omnibus to Buxton, arriving at 12 20 in time for Coaches to Whaley, Disley Stockport, Manchester, and Macclesfield.

THE OMNIBUS

WILL LEAVE

BUXTON,

ON THE ARRIVAL OF THE

CELERITY' & WONDER' COACHES,

FROM MANCHESTER,

AT 2 15

Arriving at Ladmanlow, 2 30; Hindlow, 3 10; Hurdlow, 3 30; Parsley Hay, 3 50; Friden, 4 0; Longcliff, 4 40; Hopton, 4 55; Middleton, 5 10; Steeple House, 5 15; Cromford, 5 30.

Fares from Cromford and Wirksworth, to Buxton,

Inside, 3s, 6d,: Outside, 2.s 6d.

PARCELS PUNCTUALLY DELIVERED

Railway Office Cromford, 2nd July 1856.

Notice of CHPR passenger service, 2 July 1856, front and reverse

compiled from 1852 by John Warren, an employee at the print works at Whaley Bridge. Warren, born in 1830, joined a class to learn to read and write. Members were encouraged to keep a diary of local events. There are many references to the High Peak Railway in the diary, which he maintained until 1885, and which has been privately preserved. On 19 October 1857 he noted that the first locomotive crossed the viaduct on that day. Warren's diary also records the interesting fact that on 18 November 1857 the first locomotive worked from Shallcross top to Bunsall foot.

Private traders continued to use the CHPR until January 1860 when they were given a month's notice to remove their horses from the line to enable all traffic to be worked by CHPR locomotives. Concern was expressed about people riding up and down the inclines. William Smith issued a notice on 27 August 1857 to be posted at the top and bottom of each incline. It read: 'Notice is hereby given that the Directors have ordered that no person shall be permitted to ride up or down the Inclined Plane and that any servant of the Company permitting any person to do so shall be liable to instant dismissal'. In 1859 a bone-crushing mill was opened at the foot of Hopton incline and a siding connection was proposed on 28 October.

Before the SD & WB was opened plans were prepared to extend it to Buxton. The extension was opposed by the CHPR Co without success, and the SD & WB obtained its Act in 1857[16]. It was becoming clear that the continued existence of the CHPR as an independent company was growing increasingly hazardous and the board was looking around with the idea of amalgamation with a neighbouring railway company. On 29 October 1857 it was announced that powers were to be sought to sell the line to the LNWR, MR, SD & WB or MS & L 'or to some or one of them'. In April 1858 a letter was received from the MR Co stating that it would not concur in any arrangements for working the CHPR and would oppose any such powers being given to the LNWR. It was decided on 29 April that the clauses in the bill concerning the leasing and working arrangements should be withdrawn.

The by laws as then read were to be copied and sent to the BOT for approval, and copies of the tolls were to be printed and displayed at the various stations. Also posts were to be placed at every 1/4 mile on the line as required by the General Act. On 24 June it was reported that the BOT had sanctioned the by laws. The financial affairs of the company were hardly helped by another Act in 1858[17] which gave power to raise another £60,000 in 3000 shares of £20 each and to raise £20,000 by mortgage.

After lengthy discussions the lease of the CHPR was taken up by the LNWR and was approved by that company's board on 15 December 1860. It was laid before the CHPR committee at the meeting on 22 December. On 14 February 1861 the directors were authorized to enter into arrangements with the LNWR for a minimum rent for the first year of £3,500, and £4,000 thereafter. The Lease Act of 1862[18] gave power to lease the undertaking to the LNWR for 999 years from 25 March 1861. The LNWR was to pay the CHPR Co £3,500 rent for the year ending 25 March 1862 and £4,000 for every subsequent year by half yearly instalments of £2,000 on 29 September and 25 March. Equality of treatment was to be given to traffic to or from the SD & WB and the Peak Forest Canal. To enable the CHPR to pay off a debt of £14,000 and a mortgage of £6,000 the LNWR was given powers to raise £20,000.

During this period the Midland was continuing its drive towards Manchester and in 1860 obtained an Act for an extension from Rowsley to Buxton[19]. This was opened on 1 June 1863, a remarkable achievement considering the nature of the engineering involved. The SD & WB extension was opened to Buxton two weeks later on 15 June.

The Buxton extension of the SD & WB had to pass over the CHPR in too short a distance from Whaley Bridge for it to have gained sufficient height to offer adequate headroom. The CHPR had to build a deviation to the south and to lower the line. Even this could give a maximum headroom of only 10ft 6in. On 25 February 1859 the SD & WB offered the

North London Railway 0-6-0T 7511 leaving the Hopton Wood quarry branch; Hopton tunnel is on the right *(E.R. Morten)*

Bridge carrying the Buxton line over the CHPR at Whaley Bridge, 1949. Built 1863. Clearance 13ft. Connection to Whaley Bridge station on left. *(C.J. Aston)*

Terminus of the Midland Railway branch at Wirksworth from the abandoned incline to the CHPR. On the left is an incline to a quarry. 26 August 1932 *(J.R. Hollick)*

CHPR compensation of £1,500. At the CHPR meeting on 29 April it was reported that the SD & WB were to stake out the ground and to make the cutting for the bridge. A further £3,100 was to be paid to the CHPR to enable it to make the diversion and to complete the works. The low clearance at the bridge under the SD & WB extension precluded the use of locomotives except the two Vulcan saddle tanks, Nos 6 and 7, described in the next chapter.

On 16 November 1866 the SD & WB and its Buxton extension were transferred to LNWR ownership. The Midland, finding its route beyond Buxton blocked by the SD & WB, sought the co-operation of the Manchester, Sheffield & Lincolnshire and in 1862 obtained powers to build a line from Blackwell Mill, east of Buxton, to join the projected Hyde – New Mills – Hayfield line of the MS & L at New Mills. This was completed in 1867 and at last Midland trains could reach Manchester (London Road).

The joint lease of the Manchester, Buxton, Matlock & Midlands Junction was due to expire in 1871 and, lest the LNWR should prove awkward, the Midland proposed a branch up the Ecclesbourne valley from Duffield to Wirksworth and obtained an Act for this in 1863[20]. Earlier local attempts to promote this railway had failed, but the Midland saw it as part of an alternative route, tunnelling through to Cromford and Matlock and reaching Rowsley along the west side of the Derwent valley. It was surveyed by J.S. Crossley, the MR's chief engineer. To retain its connection with the CHPR in the event of losing the Cromford link, the MR continued the line beyond Wirksworth by an extension of 61.5 chains up gradients beginning at 1 in 33 and 1 in 30, steepening to 1 in 5 at the top. Track was laid on the extension to a siding alongside the CHPR near the foot of Middleton incline, but no winding engine was installed, so the extension was unusable.

The Wirksworth branch was opened on 1 October 1867. Plans for the extension from Wirksworth to Rowsley were prepared in 1869[21]. The LNWR, realising that the Ambergate – Rowsley line would be of little use so far from its main system, and that the Midland was now in a position to by-pass it, relinquished its rights in the MBM & MJ which was absorbed by the Midland Co on 1 July 1871[22].

Thus the Midland retained its connection to the CHPR at High Peak Junction and the steeply-graded Wirksworth connection was not needed. It was still in place at the time of the CHPR inspection in October 1886, and it was marked on the Ordnance Survey map of 1898, but it was removed by 1920. Its course was still walkable in the early 1940s but was later quarried away. The question of the maintenance of High Peak Junction arose on 21 June 1872 when correspondence on the matter was discussed at a meeting of the LNWR PW, Estate & Works Committee. The Midland demanded payment of expenses for maintaining the junction under an agreement said to have been made on 2 March 1852. The charge was not enforced during the joint lease of the Matlock line. On 31 October it was stated that the LNWR had no copy of the agreement. Edward Tootal, an LNWR director living in Manchester, was asked to ascertain privately through Mr Fred Wragge what were the facts of this case[23]. There is no further reference to this matter in the minutes, so it was probably settled amicably.

NOTES

1. Derbyshire Record Office (DRO) Deposited Railway Plan (DRP) No 10 1840
2. PRO RAIL 144/5
3. DRO DRP No 7 1842
4 Cromford Canal Sale Act 1 August 1851 c 126
5 Manchester, Buxton, Matlock & Midlands Junction Railway Cromford Canal Leasing Act 17 June 1852 c 98
6 Peak Forest Canal Act 25 March 1846 c 267
7. Sheffield, Ashton & Manchester Railway Act 25 March 1846 c 268
8. MBM & MJR Act 16 July 1846 c 192; Ambergate, Nottingham & Boston & Eastern Junction Railway Act 16 July 1846 c 155
9 LNWR Act 16 July 1846 c 204
10 PRO RAIL 144/5
11 CHPR Act 26 June 1855 c 75
12 Stockport, Disley & Whaley Bridge Railway Act 31 July 1854 c 200
13 SD & WBR Act 16 July 1855 c 130
14 PRO RAIL 144/2
15 PRO RAIL 1001/34
16 SD & WB Extension Act 27 July 1857 c 98
17 CHPR Act 28 June 1858 c 61
18 CHPR (Lease) Act 30 June 1862 c 66
19 Midland Railway (Rowsley to Buxton) Act 25 May 1860 c 66
20 MR (New Lines and Additional Powers) Act 21 July 1863 c 183
21 DRO DRP No 138 1869
22 MR (Additional Powers) Act 1870 c 63
23 LNWR Special Committee Minutes 28681 and 29627, PRO RAIL 410. It is not clear who was Mr Wragge.

The train staff residing in its box at Harpur Hill Cabin *(John Holroyd)*

CROMFORD AND HIGH PEAK RAILWAY.

TIME TABLE for APRIL, 1874, and until further Notice.

Miles	Stations	1	2	3	4	5	6	7	8	9	10	11	12	13
		a m	a m	a m	a m	a m	a m	a m	a m	a m	a m	a m	a m	a m
...	High Peak Junc.	6 15	...	...	...	...	...	...	...	7 40	...	...	...	...
1	Cromford	6 25	...	...	...	...	...	...	...	7 50	...	...	...	...
1½	Sheep Pasture	...	...	6 30	...	...	...	7 25	...	...	...	...	...	8 30
2¾	Steeplehouse	...	...	6 40	...	...	...	7 35	...	...	...	...	...	8 40
3½	Middleton	...	...	6 45	6 30	...	...	7 40	7 40	...	...	...	...	8 45
5	Hopton	...	...	...	6 40	...	...	...	7 50	...	...	8 0	...	...
6¾	Buckley's Siding	...	...	...	...	...	...	...	...	...	...	8 10	...	...
7	Longcliffe	...	...	...	...	...	...	...	...	...	...	8 20	...	...
9	Bloore's Siding	...	...	...	...	...	...	...	...	...	...	8 35	...	...
10	Minninglow	...	...	...	...	...	...	...	...	...	...	8 40	...	...
12½	Friden	...	...	...	...	...	...	...	...	...	...	8 50	...	...
15	Parsley Hay	...	...	...	...	...	...	...	...	...	...	9 15	...	...
17	Hurdlow	...	...	...	...	...	...	...	...	...	...	9 30	...	...
21	Hindlow	...	...	...	...	...	...	...	...	...	...	10 0	...	...
23	Harpur Hill	...	...	...	...	...	...	...	...	...	7 40	10 15	...	...
26½	Ladmanlow	...	6 15	...	...	...	7 15	...	...	...	8 0	10 30	...	...
29¼	Bunsall	...	6 30	...	...	6 30	7 30	...	...	...	...	...	8 30	...
32¼	Shallcross	...	...	...	...	6 45	...	...	...	...	...	...	8 45	...
33¼	Whaley Bridge	...	...	...	...	...	...	...	...	...	...	...	...	...

Miles	Stations	14	15	16	17	18	19	20	21	22	23	24	25	26
		a m	a m	a m	a m	a m	a m	a m	a m	a m	a m	a m	a m	a m
...	High Peak Junc.	...	...	9 0	...	...	...	...	10 15	...	...	...	...	...
1	Cromford	...	...	9 10	...	...	...	...	10 25	...	...	...	...	...
1½	Sheep Pasture	...	...	...	...	9 45	...	...	...	...	...	11 0	...	...
2¾	Steeplehouse	...	...	...	...	9 55	...	...	...	...	...	11 10	...	...
3½	Middleton	...	9 0	...	...	10 0	...	10 15	...	...	...	11 15	...	11 10
5	Hopton	...	9 10	...	...	...	...	10 25	...	...	...	...	...	11 20
6¾	Buckley's Siding	...	...	...	...	...	...	...	...	...	...	...	...	...
7	Longcliffe	...	...	...	...	...	...	...	...	...	...	...	...	...
9	Bloore's Siding	...	...	...	...	...	...	...	...	...	...	...	...	...
10	Minninglow	...	...	...	...	...	...	...	...	...	...	...	...	...
12½	Friden	...	...	...	...	...	...	...	...	...	...	...	...	...
15	Parsley Hay	...	...	...	...	...	...	...	...	...	...	...	...	...
17	Hurdlow	...	...	...	...	...	...	...	...	...	...	...	...	...
21	Hindlow	...	...	...	...	...	...	...	...	...	...	...	...	...
23	Harpur Hill	...	...	...	...	...	...	...	...	10 30	...	...	...	...
26½	Ladmanlow	9 0	...	...	...	...	10 15	...	...	10 50	...	...	11 5	...
29¼	Bunsall	9 15	...	...	9 20	...	10 30	...	...	...	10 30	...	11 20	...
32¼	Shallcross	...	...	...	9 35	...	...	...	...	...	10 45	...	...	...
33¼	Whaley Bridge	...	...	...	...	...	...	...	...	...	...	...	...	...

Miles	Stations	27	28	29	30	31	32	33	34	35	36	37	38	39
		a m	a m	p m	p m	p m	p m	p m	p m	p m	p m	p m	p m	p m
...	High Peak Junc.	...	11 45	...	...	...	...	...	...	...	...	...	2 50	...
1	Cromford	...	12 0	...	...	...	...	...	...	...	...	...	3 0	...
1½	Sheep Pasture	...	12 15	...	...	...	1 30	...	...	...	2 30	...	...	...
2¾	Steeplehouse	...	12 35	...	...	...	1 40	...	...	...	2 40	...	...	...
3½	Middleton	...	12 40	...	...	...	1 45	...	...	2 10	2 45	...	...	...
5	Hopton	...	1 30	...	...	...	...	...	...	2 20	...	...	...	...
6¾	Buckley's Siding	...	1 40	...	...	...	...	...	...	...	...	...	...	...
7	Longcliffe	...	1 45	...	...	...	...	...	...	...	...	...	...	...
9	Bloore's Siding	...	1 55	...	...	...	...	...	...	...	...	...	...	...
10	Minninglow	...	2 0	...	...	...	...	...	...	...	...	...	...	...
12½	Friden	...	2 10	...	...	...	...	...	...	...	...	...	...	...
15	Parsley Hay	...	2 25	...	...	...	...	...	...	...	...	...	...	...
17	Hurdlow	...	2 35	...	...	...	...	...	...	...	...	...	...	...
21	Hindlow	...	3 0	...	...	...	...	...	...	...	...	...	...	...
23	Harpur Hill	...	3 15	...	1 0	...	...	...	...	...	...	...	...	...
26½	Ladmanlow	...	3 40	12 30	1 20	...	...	1 30	...	...	...	2 30	...	...
29¼	Bunsall	11 40	4 0	12 45	...	1 0	...	1 45	2 0	...	...	2 45	...	2 55
32¼	Shallcross	12 0	4 35	...	...	1 15	...	...	2 15	...	...	...	...	3 10
33¼	Whaley Bridge	...	5 10	...	...	...	...	...	...	...	...	...	...	...

Miles	Stations	40	41	42	43	44	45	46	47	48	49	50	51
		p m	p m	p m	p m	p m	p m	p m	p m	p m	p m	p m	p m
...	High Peak Junc.	...	...	3 55	...	...	...	...	4 45	...	...	5 20	...
1	Cromford	...	...	4 5	...	...	...	...	4 55	...	...	5 30	...
1½	Sheep Pasture	...	3 30	...	...	...	4 30	...	...	...	...	...	...
2¾	Steeplehouse	...	3 40	...	...	...	4 40	...	...	...	...	...	...
3½	Middleton	3 0	3 45	...	...	4 0	4 45	...	...	5 5	...	...	...
5	Hopton	3 10	...	...	...	4 10	...	...	...	5 15	...	...	...
6¾	Buckley's Siding	...	...	...	...	...	...	...	...	...	...	...	...
7	Longcliffe	...	...	...	...	...	...	...	...	...	...	...	...
9	Bloore's Siding	...	...	...	...	...	...	...	...	...	...	...	...
10	Minninglow	...	...	...	...	...	...	...	...	...	...	...	...
12½	Friden	...	...	...	...	...	...	...	...	...	...	...	...
15	Parsley Hay	...	...	...	...	...	...	...	...	...	...	...	...
17	Hurdlow	...	...	...	...	...	...	...	...	...	...	...	...
21	Hindlow	...	...	...	...	...	...	...	...	...	...	...	...
23	Harpur Hill	...	...	...	3 30	...	...	...	...	...	5 10	...	...
26½	Ladmanlow	...	...	...	3 50	...	...	4 10	...	...	5 30	...	...
29¼	Bunsall	...	...	...	...	...	...	4 35	...	...	...	...	5 20
32¼	Shallcross	...	...	...	...	...	...	...	...	...	...	...	5 35
33¼	Whaley Bridge	...	...	...	...	...	...	...	...	...	...	...	...

Miles	Stations.	1	2	3	4	5	6	7	8	9	10	11	12	13
		a m	a m	a m	a m	a m	a m	a m	a m	a m	a m	a m	a m	a m
..	Whaley Bridge	...	...	...	...	...	...	...	...	...	...	...	...	...
1½	Shallcross	...	...	...	6 0	...	...	...	...	7 30	...	...	...	...
4½	Bunsall	...	...	...	6 15	6 45	...	...	...	7 45	...	8 0	...	...
7	Ladmanlow	5 0	5 30	...	...	7 0	...	...	...	...	...	8 15	...	8 30
9¾	Harpur Hill	5 15	6 0	...	...	...	...	...	...	...	...	...	...	8 50
12½	Hindlow	5 55	...	...	...	...	...	...	...	...	...	...	...	...
16½	Hurdlow	6 10	...	...	...	...	...	...	...	...	...	...	...	...
18½	Parsley Hay	6 20	...	...	...	...	...	...	...	...	...	...	...	...
21	Friden	6 40	...	...	...	...	...	...	...	...	...	...	...	...
23½	Minninglow	6 50	...	...	...	...	...	...	...	...	...	...	...	...
24½	Bloore's Siding	6 55	...	...	...	...	...	...	...	...	...	...	...	...
26½	Longcliffe	7 20	...	...	...	...	...	...	...	...	...	...	...	...
26¾	Buckley's Siding	7 22	...	...	...	...	...	...	...	...	...	...	...	...
28½	Hopton	7 30	...	...	...	...	6 45	...	...	...	...	...	8 0	...
30	Middleton	...	...	...	...	...	6 55	6 50	...	...	7 45	...	8 10	...
30½	Steeplehouse	...	...	...	...	...	...	6 55	...	...	7 50	...	...	...
31¾	Sheep Pasture	...	...	...	...	...	...	7 0	...	...	8 0	...	...	...
32¾	Cromford	...	...	6 0	...	...	...	...	7 20	...	...	...	...	...
33¾	High Peak Junc.	...	...	6 10	...	...	...	...	7 30	...	...	...	...	...

Miles	Stations.	14	15	16	17	18	19	20	21	22	23	24	25	26
		a m	a m	a m	a m	a m	a m	a m	a m	a m	a m	a m	a m	a m
..	Whaley Bridge	...	...	...	...	...	...	...	...	...	...	...	9 20	...
1½	Shallcross	...	8 50	...	...	...	...	...	...	...	...	...	9 45	11 0
4½	Bunsall	...	9 5	...	...	9 25	...	...	...	...	...	...	10 40	11 15
7	Ladmanlow	...	...	...	...	9 40	...	...	...	...	...	...	10 55	...
9¾	Harpur Hill	...	...	...	...	...	...	...	...	...	...	...	11 15	...
12½	Hindlow	...	...	...	...	...	...	...	...	...	...	...	11 30	...
16½	Hurdlow	...	...	...	...	...	...	...	...	...	...	...	11 45	...
18½	Parsley Hay	...	...	...	...	...	...	...	...	...	...	...	12 5	...
21	Friden	...	...	...	...	...	...	...	...	...	...	...	12 20	...
23½	Minninglow	...	...	...	...	...	...	...	...	...	...	...	12 30	...
24½	Bloore's Siding	...	...	...	...	...	...	...	...	...	...	...	12 35	...
26½	Longcliffe	...	...	...	...	...	...	...	...	...	...	...	12 50	...
26¾	Buckley's Siding	...	...	...	...	...	...	...	...	...	...	...	12 55	...
28½	Hopton	...	...	...	9 15	...	...	...	10 30	...	11 25	...	1 0	...
30	Middleton	...	...	9 0	9 25	...	...	10 15	10 40	...	11 35	11 30	2 0	...
30½	Steeplehouse	...	...	9 5	...	...	...	10 20	...	...	...	11 35	2 5	...
31¾	Sheep Pasture	...	...	9 15	...	...	...	10 30	...	...	...	11 45	2 15	...
32¾	Cromford	8 40	...	...	...	...	10 0	...	...	11 10	...	...	2 30	...
33¾	High Peak Junc.	8 50	...	...	...	...	10 10	...	...	11 20	...	...	2 45	...

Miles	Stations.	27	28	29	30	31	32	33	34	35	36	37	38	39
		a m	a m	p m	p m	p m	p m	p m	p m	p m	p m	p m	p m	p m
..	Whaley Bridge	...	...	...	...	...	...	...	...	...	...	...	...	...
1½	Shallcross	...	...	12 30	...	...	1 30	...	...	...	2 25	...	...	...
4½	Bunsall	...	11 30	12 45	...	1 0	1 45	...	2 0	...	2 40	...	3 0	...
7	Ladmanlow	11 10	11 45	...	...	1 15	...	2 0	2 15	...	...	...	3 15	...
9¾	Harpur Hill	11 30	...	...	...	...	...	2 20	...	...	...	...	...	...
12½	Hindlow	...	...	...	...	...	...	...	...	...	...	...	...	...
16½	Hurdlow	...	...	...	...	...	...	...	...	...	...	...	...	...
18½	Parsley Hay	...	...	...	...	...	...	...	...	...	...	...	...	...
21	Friden	...	...	...	...	...	...	...	...	...	...	...	...	...
23½	Minninglow	...	...	...	...	...	...	...	...	...	...	...	...	...
24½	Bloore's Siding	...	...	...	...	...	...	...	...	...	...	...	...	...
26½	Longcliffe	...	...	...	...	...	...	...	...	...	...	...	...	...
26¾	Buckley's Siding	...	...	...	...	...	...	...	...	...	...	...	...	...
28½	Hopton	...	...	...	...	...	...	...	...	2 25	...	...	...	3 15
30	Middleton	...	...	...	12 45	...	...	...	...	2 35	...	3 0	...	3 25
30½	Steeplehouse	...	...	...	12 50	...	...	...	...	...	...	3 5	...	...
31¾	Sheep Pasture	...	...	...	1 0	...	...	...	...	...	...	3 15	...	...
32¾	Cromford	...	...	...	...	...	...	...	...	...	...	...	...	...
33¾	High Peak Junc.	...	...	...	...	...	...	...	...	...	...	...	...	...

Miles	Stations.	40	41	42	43	44	45	46	47	48	49	50	51
		p m	p m	p m	p m	p m	p m	p m	p m	p m	p m	p m	p m
..	Whaley Bridge	...	...	...	...	...	...	...	...	...	...	...	...
1½	Shallcross	3 25	...	...	...	...	...	...	4 50	...	...	...	...
4½	Bunsall	3 40	...	...	...	4 15	...	...	5 5	5 0	...	...	...
7	Ladmanlow	...	...	...	...	4 30	...	4 10	...	5 15	...	...	...
9¾	Harpur Hill	...	...	...	...	...	...	4 30	...	...	...	...	...
12½	Hindlow	...	...	...	...	...	...	...	...	...	...	...	...
16½	Hurdlow	...	...	...	...	...	...	...	...	...	...	...	...
18½	Parsley Hay	...	...	...	...	...	...	...	...	...	...	...	...
21	Friden	...	...	...	...	...	...	...	...	...	...	...	...
23½	Minninglow	...	...	...	...	...	...	...	...	...	...	...	...
24½	Bloore's Siding	...	...	...	...	...	...	...	...	...	...	...	...
26½	Longcliffe	...	...	...	...	...	...	...	...	...	...	...	...
26¾	Buckley's Siding	...	...	...	...	...	...	...	...	...	...	...	...
28½	Hopton	...	...	...	4 15	...	...	...	...	...	...	...	5 20
30	Middleton	...	...	4 0	4 25	...	...	...	...	...	5 0	...	5 30
30½	Steeplehouse	...	...	4 5	...	...	...	...	...	...	5 5	...	...
31¾	Sheep Pasture	...	...	4 15	...	...	...	...	...	...	5 15	...	...
32¾	Cromford	...	3 40	...	...	...	4 30	...	...	...	...	5 5	...
33¾	High Peak Junc.	...	3 50	...	...	...	4 40	...	...	...	...	5 15	...

REGULATIONS FOR WORKING BETWEEN LADMANLOW AND HARPUR HILL.

The Line between Ladmanlow and Harpur Hill must be worked by an Engine Staff lettered L. & HH. All Engines passing between these points must carry the Staff, with the Exception of the 5.0 a.m., and 10.55 a.m. Trains from Ladmanlow, and the 10.15 a.m., and 3.15 p.m. Trains from Harpur Hill. The Enginemen in charge of these four Trains must see the Staff at the Starting points immediately before proceeding on their journey.

At Ladmanlow between the Buxton Lime Co.'s Branch and the Coal Siding, the Line must be worked by Signals from Ladmanlow; and Engines must not pass over this length at a greater Speed than Four Miles per Hour. The Arm on that side of the Signal Post which is nearest to the Main Line of Rails, is the Signal for Engines from Whaley Bridge to Cromford, or Cromford to Whaley Bridge. The Arm on the side of the Signal Post, away from the Main Line, is the Signal for Engines between Ladmanlow and the Coal Branch. An Engineman from the Main Line must give One Whistle, and from the Branch or Coal Siding Two Whistles, and must not proceed beyond the Signal until it is lowered.

McCorquodale & Co., Printers, London—Works, Newton.

4. Motive Power

The nine stationary engines supplied by the Butterley Co were of three sizes: Cromford, Sheep Pasture, Middleton, Bunsall Upper and Lower and Shallcross were described in the Butterley 'Furnace Accounts' as 'Two Steam Engines of 20hp each'. The Hopton and Hurdlow engines were 'Two Steam Engines of 10hp each'. The Whaley Bridge engine was described as '10 horses double power' which, in this instance, meant two engines of 5hp each. Each cylinder, beam and crank were described as one engine. As an example, the cost of a large engine, dated 1 December 1829, was:

Two Steam Engines 20hp each for the Cromford Upper Plane	2000	0	0
Coal rake and picker for Do	2	13	3
Chain wheel for Do	211	4	8
Models (patterns) for machinery	65	17	6
Floor bearers, covering plates, indicator for Do	90	12	2½
Pipes, cistern	108	11	11½
Break and Winding out gear for Do	42	0	0
	£2521	19	7

The cost of a smaller engine, for Hopton for example, dated 2 June 1830, was:

Two Steam Engines 10hp each	1200	0	0
Coal rake and picker for Do	2	2	0
Pipes	8	2	5
Floor bearers, covering plates	55	11	0
Indicator	10	0	0
Large chain wheel, etc	101	9	4½
Winding out gear	12	3	6
Break	23	1	0
Horizontal and vertical pulleys	43	19	4½
Guide pulley 20in diameter – 3 pulleys	10	10	6
Turn pulley, etc	41	19	6½
Models for machinery for plane	38	2	0
	£1547	2	10½

The total outlay for the six large and two smaller engines, machinery and other items, and including chain, pulleys and brake for the Whaley Bridge incline (dated May and June 1831), amounted to £23,852 1s 2d. The small engine for the Whaley incline appeared in the accounts, in August and September 1833 as:

A steam Engine 10 horses double power	£600	0	0
Brasses, handrail for Do	9	17	2
Pinions, winding out gear	29	4	2
4½in pipes and bracket	28	17	2
	£667	18	6

In addition to all this outlay was the cost of the engine houses which formed an integral part of the engine structures, boilers, chimneys, pulleys (which had to be mounted on separate stone blocks between the rails) and numerous other accessories.

The six large engines (considered here as complete two-cylinder machines) had cylinders about 23-25in diameter and 5ft stroke, and worked on the double-acting condensing principle. No record has been found of the dimensions of the Hopton and Hurdlow engines but, as they went out of use in 1877 and 1869, this is not surprising. Steam pressure was originally 2½psi, increased later to 5psi. The piston rods drove the 16ft 3in long beams through James Watt parallel motion. The boiler was supplied by a feed pump operated from the beam. Both Cornish and Lancashire boilers appear to have been used. (Cornish boilers have one furnace flue, Lancashire two).

The crankshaft carried a flywheel 16ft 2in diameter, cast in two sections and keyed onto the shaft, also the two eccentrics for the valve gear, and a pinion 5ft pitch diameter with 75 teeth. This engaged with a spur wheel 13ft 9½in pitch diameter below it, secured to the driving pulley, or winding drum which had two grooves 14ft 1in diameter. It also carried a brake drum on which worked a band brake with wooden brake blocks. An idler pulley, also 14ft diameter, was mounted above the crankshaft.

Steam distribution was by slide valves with 7in travel. The valve gear was normally operated automatically with a fixed cut-off. By means of two large levers the valves could be disengaged from the eccentrics and operated manually. The manual function could be used at starting with full valve opening and also for brief reversing movements. The condensers were mounted below the cylinders and in front horizontally and were placed in cold water cisterns. These condensed the steam from above or below the pistons, creating a partial vacuum, speeded up by spraying cold water into the condensers, so that the driving force on the piston was atmospheric pressure. An air pump, operated from each beam, pumped condensed steam and air from the condensers and into hot wells which contained the boiler feed pumps.

The chain or rope, on entering the winding house, passed over the top of the driving pulley, round it for three quarters of a circle, up over the upper pulley, down and round half the drive pulley again, then up and round three quarters of the upper pulley and outside again. So the chain or rope passed 1¼ times round the driving pulley and was curved in one direction only.

The pinion on the crank axle was arranged to slide into or out of mesh with the spur wheel, so that when the descending loads were greater than the ascending the engine was disengaged and only the brake was used. Tension was maintained by a 9ft 6in diameter straining wheel at the foot of the incline. The wheel was mounted on a carriage which moved in a pit 24ft long. Chains gripped the driving wheels by friction only; the links of hand-made chains, although made with a gauge, could not be relied upon to fit into a sprocket.

From the Butterley accounts it appeared that the engines needed various renewals fairly soon. Examples are: on 2 January 1838 '1 chain wheel, set of arms and segments, 1 shaft and 1 pinion for 20H engine, Cromford plain' £175 17s 2d; on 26 September 'Metallic pistons fitted complete for 10 and 20H engines' £34 0s 0d; and on 21 August

'Metallic piston fitted completed for 20H engine' £21 5s 0d. Further pistons were required for large and smaller engines in 1840, 1841 and 1843, also new crankshaft and slide valves. There were also numerous accounts for 'gangwaggon wheels'.

Originally chains were obtained from the Butterley Company. The account books record, on 10 July 1829: '2 Chains for Cromford Inclined Plane. Lower 8T 4c 2q 12 lb £384 1s 8d; Upper 6T 19c 2q 16 lb £325 16s 8d, total £709 18s 4d'; on 18 August: '1 Chain for Middleton Plane, £387 12s 6d'; on 16 April 1830: 'Large chain for Hopton Plane £176 4s 2d'; on 19 March 1831; 'Chain for Hurdlow Plane £271 16s 8d, for Buxton Upper Plane £843 10s 5d, Buxton Lower Plane £802 0s 0d' and 'Chain for Shallcross Plane 9T 17c 3q 23 lb £461 17s 11d'. Finally, on 26 May 1831: 'Chain for Whaley Plane, 500yd long with 6 piercing links, 2T 5c 1q 23 lb £106 1s 3d'. What were 'piercing links'?

Throughout the 137 year history of the CHPR upkeep of chains and later ropes on the inclines was a constant concern. On 20 January 1836 Leonard wrote to the Coalbrookdale Co for prices of chains made of iron bar of the following fractions of an inch: 15/16, 13/16, 3/4, 11/16, 5/8, 9/16, 1/2, 7/16 and 3/8. He explained that there was nearly 7 miles or about 80 tons of chain in constant use and that they would shortly have to renew about 2 miles of 3/4 or 11/16 inch size. He asked for 5 or 6cwt of 11/16 in to be sent immediately for making shackles for connecting the two ends of the chains when serviced. On 18 March 1836 he ordered 3 tons of 3/4in best chain iron from the Coalbrookdale Co and on 6 June he wrote to them again:

'By direction of the Committee of Management of the Cromford & High Peak Railway I have paid into the hands of Messrs Arkwright & Co, Wirksworth, the sum of £50 6s 7d who will transmit the same for your use into the hands of Messrs Darby & Co, Bankers, Coalbrookdale.

Please prepare 3 or 4 tons more of 3/4 best chain iron similar to last'.

Another order for chain iron, dated 21 December 1849 and addressed to Messrs Mold, specified 2T 10c 'to complete order'. The length of the links was to be 13in and the chain was to be supplied in sections of 12 links, 13ft long, or 13 links, 14ft 1in long. An order for sufficient iron for a new chain for Hopton incline was made to Barrows & Hall on 9 June 1860.

Besides chain iron the Coalbrookdale Co also supplied boiler plates. On 13 July 1837 Leonard asked the company to supply 1 or 1½ tons of best boiler plates, in about 2 weeks, to measure 6ft 0in x 2ft 1½ in x 5/16 in. Thickness was 'not to exceed' 5/16 in. Surely this should have been the minimum thickness. From this it appears that the CHPR made its own boilers for the stationary engines. As the boilers worked at only a little above atmospheric pressure, 5/16in plates would be thick enough, but they could hardly be less. Allowing for canal transport from Coalbrookdale, they must have worked with speed to deliver the plates in 2 weeks.

On 7 August 1837 Leonard wrote to the Butterley Co following an accident on the Cromford Upper incline caused by the breaking of a chain wheel. A new one was ordered, to be cast in four parts with the arms, or spokes, cast in two parts, to enable it to be taken into the engine house, and requiring nothing more than bolting together.

The leaky state of the stationary engine reservoirs was brought to the notice of the board on 22 June 1859. Hopton reservoir was to be repaired immediately and a new one of the same size as the existing one was to be constructed at the Sheep Pasture engine, provided the land could be obtained.

The early locomotive history of the CHPR is both obscure and confused, with conflicting details which defy reconciliation. The extract quoted from Jessop's report of September 1824, and Section 2 of the 1825 Act, make it clear that the use of steam locomotives was considered from the beginning. At first the line was worked entirely by stationary engines and horses. The CHPR bought its first locomotive in 1833 from Robert Stephenson & Co, Newcastle upon Tyne (RS No 45). It was a 0-4-0 (at this date almost certainly a tender locomotive) and was name *Peak*. It had 12 x 16in cylinders and 5ft wheels.

The *Derby Mercury,* on 31 December 1834, carried a report of a locomotive assembled in the small workshop at Cromford under the direction of John Leonard. The report describes how it was tried on 13 December between Sheep Pasture top and Middleton foot hauling one wagon containing 16 persons at a maximum speed of 12mph, and a 3 ton load at 10mph. This may have been the Robert Stephenson locomotive, but the delay of a year is puzzling. It is made no clearer by another report in the *Derby Mercury* on 24 June 1835 which describes a journey on the line by the CHPR proprietors. At Middleton top 'Mr Gell's experimental locomotive took them forward, at 7 to 8mph owing to the engine being overloaded'. Presumably it worked only to Hopton foot. Philip Gell was a CHPR director. This again may have been the Robert Stephenson locomotive, which was probably CHPR No 1.

In 1835 Edward Bury & Co of Liverpool supplied a 2-2-0 tender locomotive which became CHPR No 2. It may have been obtained second hand. Cylinders were 12 x 18in, driving wheels 4ft 8in, leading wheels 3ft 0in; length of engine 18ft 6in; engine and tender 32ft 3in; weight 9½ tons. In 1860 this locomotive replaced horses on the High Peak Junction – Sheep Pasture foot section. In June 1864 the boiler was fitted with a new copper firebox at Longsight, Manchester, and it returned to the CHPR to the Sheep Pasture foot section where it worked from 26 January to 10 April 1865. It was then transferred to the Hopton top – Hurdlow foot section and remained there until 17 March 1868. Afterwards it worked on the Sheep Pasture top and bottom sections. When taken into LNWR stock in November 1871 it was numbered 2039 but a month

Bury 2-2-0, originally CHPR No 2, rebuilt as saddle tank c 1873. Scrapped 1876

later it became 1942 in the duplicate list of locomotives. Later it was fitted at Crewe with a saddle tank and the weight became 5 tons 4cwt + 8 tons 14cwt, total 13 tons 18cwt. In May 1873 it was transferred to Crewe Locomotive Machinery Department and given the letter 'B' (see photograph) and it shunted at Crewe works until it was scrapped in May 1876.

The next report of a locomotive appeared in the *Derby Mercury* on 3 February 1841 and the *Railway Times* on 6 February, p127. The locomotive was again built under the direction of Mr Leonard, but whether or not at Cromford is not stated. It was tried on the Sheep Pasture top section about 20-30 January 1841. The only details given about it are that it had outside cylinders level with the wheels, that it weighed $5^3/_4$ tons, and cost about £400. This may have been CHPR No 3. The report added: 'The intention is to construct, as speedily as possible, two more engines to work the two 12-mile levels between Hopton and Buxton at a rate of 10 to 12mph'.

At this period various railway managements were becoming interested in Brunel's notorious atmospheric system of propulsion. It was installed on the Kingstown & Dalkey line south of Dublin and was set in operation in March 1844. News about it spread to the CHPR; on 7 March Leonard was 'allowed to proceed to Dublin' to examine the system and to report on how far, in his opinion, it might be used on the inclines. Evidently Leonard was not impressed because it was not mentioned again.

Under the heading 'Locomotive Power' a note in the minutes on 19 May 1842 records: 'an engine to be set to work on the summit level as soon as ready, operation to be then suspended until annual meeting'. On 7 May 1843 John Leonard was asked 'to build a suitable shed for the reception of the locomotive engine and tender at the Hopton Incline'.

It was reported at the meeting on 30 January 1856 that a locomotive now ran from the top of Buxton Incline to the Hurdlow Incline, about 12 miles, and another engine had been purchased and would shortly be at work. This would make it possible to dispense with a number of horses. The report to the CHPR directors on 27 February 1856, mentioned earlier, adds to the confusion: 'One locomotive at work on the High Level and another, recently bought, under alteration to make it suited to cast-iron rails. At present unsuitable because of excess weight'.

William Needham reported on 26 March 1857 that he had been in touch with Messrs Neilson concerning purchase of another locomotive and that Mr Blenkinsop was about to visit Glasgow to deal with the matter. Purchase of the engine was agreed upon, but on 30 July the chairman reported that he had communicated with Neilson about the new engine and he believed they were willing to take it back upon receiving orders for two others of less power and weight. Such arrangements were to be made.

Locomotive power is mentioned several times in the company minutes at this period. On 24 September 1857 the secretary was asked to advertise for the hire or purchase of two locomotives of the size and specification submitted to him, and on 29 October Broome was authorized to purchase an engine which was then on the Eastern Counties Railway for not more than £500. No such engine was purchased. A note in Warren's diary recorded the first use of a locomotive between Shallcross top and Bunsall foot on 18 November 1857.

Instructions were issued on 28 May 1858 that engine sheds were to be built at Ladmanlow and Shallcross and tenders were to be obtained from builders. Ladmanlow became the principal CHPR shed until the line was closed from there to Shallcross in 1892 when it was closed and demolished.

At the meeting on 10 September 1858 the engineer stressed the great advantage to traffic if locomotives worked throughout instead of horses, but the capital of the company was not sufficient. It was proposed that a private company should be formed to raise funds for the purpose. Another proposal was that the redundant stationary engines at No 1 incline (Cromford) and No 7 (Bunsall Lower) should be sold and the money received should be paid to the Butterley Co.

Three weeks later, on 1 October, it was stated that the directors were about to arrange for hire of locomotives to work between Hopton and Ladmanlow. On 29 October the following had agreed to find the necessary capital for the construction of two new locomotives.

Peter Arkwright	£250
John Cruso	£250
John Wright	£200
Thomas Gisborne	£100
George Goodwin	£100
Philip Hubbersty	£100
	£1000

There is no record of the disposal of the redundant stationary engines but on 20 March 1861 the company accepted offers of £25 each from Francis Barton for 'old materials' in the Cromford engine house and from the Buxton Lime Co for the Bunsall Lower engine house. By then the engines must have been removed. The engine houses were probably dismantled soon afterwards for building materials.

Locomotive No 4, a 0-6-0 saddle tank built at Cromford in 1859, began work on 1 June.[1] No 5, also built at Cromford, was similar; it began work on 2 January 1860. Both had outside cylinders 10 x 12in; wheels 3ft 0in; were 21ft long and weighed 12¾ tons. No 4 was fitted with a new copper firebox in 1866. In November 1871 it became LNWR 2040, and 1943 in December 1871. It was transferred to the Locomotive Machinery Department and lettered 'D' in March 1877. In 1878 it was used on ballast work in the construction of the line from Bettws-y-Coed to Blaenau Ffestiniog and the accompanying photograph shows it engaged on this work at Dolwyddelan. It was scrapped on 23 May 1882.

No 5 was sent to Crewe on 26 November 1868 to have a new copper firebox fitted and was further rebuilt in October 1869. On 29 October it was returned to Whaley Bridge and it later worked at Cromford until 1871. It became LNWR 2041 in November 1871, and 1944 in December. In November 1876 it became 'C' in the Locomotive Machinery Department. Its final disposal date is not known.

The next two locomotives, Nos 6 and 7, were 0-6-0 saddle tanks built by Vulcan Foundry in 1860 (VF 435-6). They had outside cylinders 9 x 15in; wheels 3ft 0in; wheelbase 8ft 6in. They were 17ft 6¾in long over buffer beams, 21ft 9in over buffers. Weight was 14 tons 9cwt. With a height of only 9ft 10½in they were able to work under the LNWR bridge at Whaley Bridge. The heating surface was: tubes 240.3ft^2, firebox 34ft^2, boiler pressure 100psi. Their form can be seen in the diagram[2].

No 6 was delivered to Ladmanlow on 21 March 1860 and worked between there and Hurdlow top. It had a new copper firebox in April 1863, and from 4 December 1863 to 2 March 1864 was on loan to Buxton Lime Co. Until the opening of the Hurdlow deviation (see Ch 6) it worked on various sections and then, on 12 October 1869, it worked through between Ladmanlow and Hopton top. It became LNWR 2040 in November 1871, 1945 in December, and was withdrawn in March 1879.

No 7 was also delivered to Ladmanlow, in April 1860. It received a new copper firebox on 30 June 1862 and on 8 April 1864 the boiler was sent to Longsight for another new firebox, fitted in October. After being used as a spare engine, from 5 September 1868 to January 1869, it worked between Ladmanlow and Hurdlow top then, after the deviation was opened, through to Hopton top. It

0-6-0ST, former CHPR No 4, built at Cromford 1859, as LNWR 'D' at Dolwyddelan on construction of the Bettws-y-Coed – Blaenau Ffestiniog line in 1878

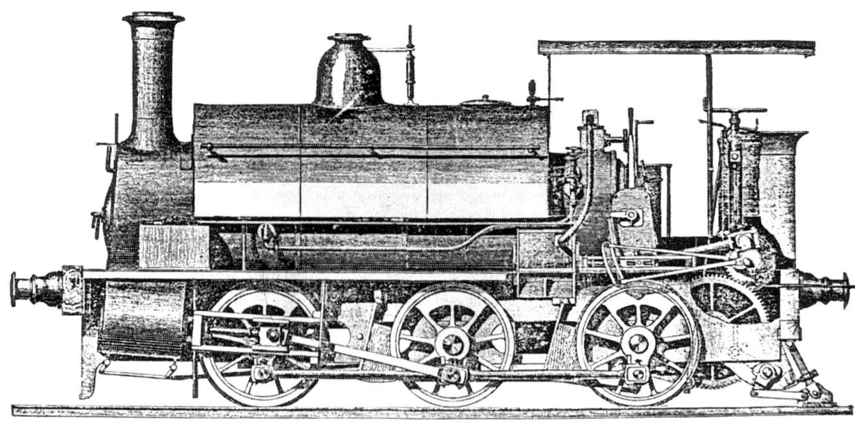

0-6-0ST with handyside patent winch as used on Hopton incline.
(Locomotive 15/7/1933)

became LNWR 2043 in November 1871 and 1946 in December. On 7 March 1879 it was transferred to the Locomotive Machinery Department and lettered 'F' and in November 1879 it was sold for £225 to a 'Mr Peak' of Tunstall, Staffordshire, possibly 'Peake's Tileries', Tunstall[3].

The parliamentary returns in 1860 and 1861, the last years of separate returns, give the locomotive stock as seven. A report in July 1862 mentions six locomotives in stock 'not counting the one worn out and replaced by one from Crewe'. On 1 May 1863 No 1 was transferred to the workshop at Cromford for driving machinery and the old shop engine was sent to Crewe. By the mid 1860s locomotives were in use on all the levels except between Whaley Bridge and Shallcross foot and Middleton top to Hopton foot where horses were still used. The half-way post was on the Middleton side of the tunnel. An article in *Chamber's Journal*, 2 May 1868, describes how this stretch was the scene of races between drivers of horses if another train could be seen approaching in the opposite direction, the first at the half-way post having the privilege of proceeding.

The first LNWR locomotive to work on the CHPR was outside-cylinder 2-4-0 side tank No 404 (RS 1082 of 1857), ex Birkenhead Railway No 2. From 1863 the LNWR began to transfer 'Crewe Goods' 2-4-0s to the CHPR. First to arrive was No 11. Others were 105 (rebuilt to 2-4-0 tank March 1857), 107, 170, 172, 238 (tank from March 1871), 298 (tank from October 1870), and 303 (tank from August 1870). In 1866-7 two Sharp 2-2-2s, ex Birkenhead Railway 21 and 22, LNWR 316 and 285, worked on the line.

At a meeting of the Locomotive Committee on 20 October 1871 the solicitor pointed out that the five engines taken over from the CHPR had never been incorporated in the Crewe stock so that the company possessed five engines more than appear in the accounts. It was resolved that these engines should be added to the stock in the Crewe books and renewed with the batch of engines to be replaced on revenue account. The old engines, nos 2, 4, 5, 6 and 7, were to continue to work the CHPR under duplicate stock numbers. In November 1871 they were taken into LNWR stock.

Several single-wheelers were used for short periods; they would be satisfactory with the light trains on the level sections. An interesting visitor in August 1863 was the ex Sandy & Potton Railway 0-4-0 well tank *Shannon*, built by George England, London, in 1857 and numbered LNWR 1104 in 1862. For two weeks it was stationed at Ladmanlow, but it was returned to Longsight as unsuitable. In 1878 it was sold to the Wantage Tramway, on which it worked until the line was closed in 1947. It is now preserved at Didcot.

Another interesting visitor was former Cockermouth & Workington 0-4-2T No 3 (Hawthorn 1849). As LNWR 1147 it worked on the CHPR for four years from July 1867. Three former St Helens Railway locomotives were used on the CHPR in 1865-9: 0-4-0 tender, ex SHR No 6 *John Smith* as LNWR 1372, renumbered 1197 in September 1865; 2-4-0, ex SHR No 9 *Swallow*, as LNWR 1375 and renumbered 1200 in November 1866; and 2-4-0, ex SHR 24 *Alma* as LNWR 1390, 1125 from November 1866. The first was originally a Bury engine, completely rebuilt in 1855. The last two were originally Liverpool & Manchester engines built at Edge Hill in 1841-5.

There are many references to maintenance of the stationary engines. In February 1856 Mr Edward Reynolds, engineer of the Butterley Co, inspected the engines and reported on them on 25 February. An interesting feature of his report is his recommendation to fit reversing gear to the engines at Sheep Pasture top and Bunsall top. This was the period when these inclines were about to be converted to single inclines with one engine at the head of each. The reversing gear probably referred to the manual function mentioned earlier.

At Sheep Pasture the boilers were worn out and a new piston was wanted. The cost of a new boiler 20ft long, 6ft 3in diameter, with two 2ft 6in flues, shell and tubes $^{5}/_{16}$in thick and ends $^{7}/_{16}$in, including delivery and erection was £560. A new boiler was also needed at Middleton; one cylinder had a hole in

'Crewe Goods 2-4-0 leaving the north end of Buxton tunnel c 1880. This section was abandoned in 1892.
From a wash drawing by Brian Fawcett

it and the other needed a new bottom; cost £680. The Hopton boiler was described as 'very bad'; £260. At Hurdlow the cylinders needed reboring, both valve casings were broken and one boiler was 'very bad'; £270. At Bunsall top another new boiler was required, also new cylinders and covers; £600. Although Reynolds did not inspect the Whaley Bridge engine he allowed £150 for repairs.

The stationary engine chimneys at Bunsall, Hurdlow, Hopton and Middleton, after 30 years of battering by the wild upland weather, were in need of repairs. On 16 June 1864 Smith submitted a tender from Campbell & Co, £66 13s 0d, including all expenses and charges, and this was accepted. The new boiler at Bunsall top was the subject of a Locomotive Committee minute on 15 February 1865 when Captain Huish recommended that as it was of similar pattern to those in the locomotive department it should be made at Crewe.

On 22-23 July 1862 Charles Mason, assistant manager of the LNWR, made a tour of inspection of the CHPR from Whaley Bridge to Cromford. His report to the general manager has survived. He noted that the Whaley engine was out of order because of mining subsidence under the engine house foundations. A note in the margin of the report added that the incline was being worked by horse. A report to the LNWR board, read on 1 April 1863, recommended that repairs and rebuilding of the foundations of the engine on the Whaley incline should not be proceeded with and that a horizontal wheel with 'break'[4] should be substituted. The engine and boilers were to be removed if and when they could be used elsewhere.

An interesting experiment was carried out on the CHPR in 1863-4. On 20 November 1862 John Barraclough Fell applied to the LNWR for permission to experiment on one of the CHPR inclines with a centre-rail locomotive to establish the feasibility of the system for the projected railway over the Mont Cenis Pass between France and Italy. The LNWR Special Committee minutes on 3 September 1863 recorded that permission was granted, provided that Fell paid all the costs.

On 24 August Warren recorded in his diary that work had begun on 'altring the in Cline plain of the High Peak Real way at Whaley Bridge to work a Engin up the plain Called the all pine, Maid at Birkinhead on a new princepel'. (sic) From this it appears that the locomotive was named *Alpine*.

Sheep Pasture engine, converted from old DX 0-6-0 chassis. Brought into use 10 February 1884 and at work until replaced by electric power in 1964

Rebuilt 'Crewe Goods' 2-4-0T 1839 at Middleton top. Formerly No 216, built July 1852. Rebuilt to tank December 1866. Renumbered 1839 May 1883 and 3061 in February 1887.

It was built by Brassey at Canada Works, Birkenhead, and was tested on the incline at Whaley Bridge from September 1863 to February 1864. At this period the Whaley incline was undergoing reconstruction, as explained earlier, and it would be a simple matter to lay in the additional rails or rail to the gauge of 3ft 7⁵/₁₆in (1.1m) and the Fell centre rail consisting of a double-headed rail on its side, with its centre 7½in above the running rails. Apparently there were two series of trials, first on the Whaley Bridge incline, 180yd at 1 in 13½ and later, in January 1864, on that and another incline of 150yd at 1 in 12 with reverse curves of 2½ and 3 chains radius. This was most likely in the space between the CHPR and the Buxton line on the Shallcross side of the bridge under the LNWR[5]. According to the French engineer Desbrière[6] the locomotive had a unique feature, a steam jet used to direct sand onto each side of the centre rail just ahead of the leading pair of gripping wheels. If this is so then it antedated by 22 years the first use of steam sanding on the Midland Railway in 1886.

The locomotive had two outside cylinders 11¾ x 18in driving the four coupled wheels which were 2ft 3in diameter with a wheelbase of 5ft 3in, and two inside cylinders 11 x 10in driving the four horizontal wheels which were 1ft 4in diameter with a wheelbase of 1ft 7in. These wheels were pressed against the centre rail with a force of 16 tons by a mechanism of levers and bevel wheels worked from the footplate. The weight of the engine in working order was 16 tons. The locomotive worked traffic up and down the incline and around the adjacent sharp curves. In a letter in *The Engineer* of 22 January 1864, p51, Mr A. A. Alexander of Millwall Ironworks, London, claimed to have designed it. The experiment is described in detail by Captain Tyler[7]. A reference in the *Buxton Advertiser* on 2 January 1864 and *The Engineer* on 22 January leave no doubt that the tests were carried out between Shallcross Yard and Whaley Bridge.

From the list of chains and ropes we learn that a new chain, 470yd long, was installed on the Whaley incline on 6 July 1864. The original chain, installed on 24 August 1838 was 433yd long. On 25-26 October 1886 a group of LNWR officers including the chief civil engineer Francis Stevenson, and chief mechanical engineer Francis Webb, made a tour of inspection of the CHPR. Their report stated that traffic between the canal wharf at Whaley Bridge and Shallcross yard was entirely hauled by horses which also performed some of the shunting at Shallcross. It was agreed to replace the horses by 'a small engine (second size)' and to ease the gradient on the incline. These suggestions were never put into effect, but a horse capstan was installed at the head of the incline, possibly soon afterwards. It was certainly in use by April 1891 because it appears as a 'windlass' in a list of the inclines and gradients signed by G. E. Mawby, district superintendent, Manchester. Horses were still used when this section was closed in 1952. At Bunsall top new air pumps and condensers, made by the Butterley Co, were installed in November 1867.

In September 1868 John Ramsbottom, then the LNWR locomotive superintendent, was asked to inspect the CHPR and to consider the most economical method of working the line. His report, dated 12 January 1869,[8] outlined repairs to be carried out on the six remaining stationary engines and their boilers. At Shallcross the cast-iron beams supporting the upper main pulley were to be replaced by wrought-iron girders, and a light roof was to be erected over the boilers, one of which was to be repaired; estimated cost was £300. At Bunsall an additional boiler was to be 'put down' and one repaired; £720. Here too the cast-iron girders were to be replaced by wrought-iron. The Hurdlow engine, then just made redundant by the deviation line (to be mentioned later), was to be used for spare parts. The cylinders of the Hopton engine were in bad condition and were to be renewed in the spring at a cost of £180. New boilers were wanted at Middleton, and new cylinders if the existing ones could not be rebored; £840. Sheep Pasture required new boilers and stronger beams; £625.

At a meeting of the Locomotive Committee at Crewe on 19 February 1869 it was recommended that repairs to the stationery engines at Bunsall and Shallcross inclines, and also the engine and shed and cottages at Ladmanlow should be proceeded with but that work on the Hopton, Middleton and Sheep Pasture engines should be referred to the chairman for further consideration. At the following meeting, at Wolverton on 12 March, it was decided to proceed with the repairs.

At Middleton the engine was stopped for repairs on 7 August 1869. A note in an incline notebook states that on 9 August a locomotive started working, probably adapted to work as a winding engine. This was during the period of single-line working. The engine was fitted with new cylinders and valve gear and resumed work on 7 February 1870.

Ramsbottom's report also referred to the locomotives at work on the line, as follows:

Shallcross top to Bunsall foot: ex St Helens Railway 2-4-0 No 1125

Bunsall top to Hurdlow top: 'Crewe Goods' No 303; Ramsbottom 0-4-0 saddle tank No 1363; CHPR 0-6-0St No 7.

Hurdlow foot to Hopton top: ex SHR 0-4-0 No 1197, described as carrying a saddle tank holding 420 gallons and a lengthened footplate and coal bunker, bringing the total weight to 23tons 12cwt. He recommended rebuilding it to run with an old Crewe tender, reducing the weight to 19tons 12cwt, to work the 24 miles from Hopton top to Bunsall top.

Middleton foot to Sheep Pasture top: CHPR 0-6-0ST No 6

Sheep Pasture foot to High Peak Junction: Bury 2-2-0, CHPR No 2

Horses were used on the Whaley Bridge to Shallcross foot and Hopton foot to Middleton top sections.

Horse capstan at top of Whaley incline *(E.R. Morten)*

LNWR 2-4-0T on Hopton incline between June 1889 when it was numbered 3049 and June 1894 when it was scrapped

2-4-0T 3061 at Middleton top with a group of CHPR employees between February 1887 when numbered 3061 and August 1894 when withdrawn.

The boilers at Hopton were becoming worn out, and pressure was dropped from $2^1/_2$ to $1^1/_2$psi. This could have been the reason for experimenting with locomotive power.

In 1876 a trial was carried out by Handyside (Steep Gradient) Co Ltd of Derby with a 0-6-0 saddle tank fitted with a steam winch. It could be described as a mobile winding engine. It would ascend part of the incline, paying out about 200 yards of rope; it was then clipped to the rails and the train was hauled up by the winch. The train was then clipped to the rails, the locomotive moved on up the incline, and the operation was repeated. The illustration[9] shows the first locomotive to be built under the Handyside patent in 1875 which was used successfully on a gradient of 1 in 10 in the construction of Avonmouth dock. The engine tried on the CHPR was the second, built in 1876. This had several modifications, to the gripper brake and other details.

The engine was built by Fox Walker & Co, Atlas Works, Bristol. It had a wheelbase of 9ft $8^1/_2$ in; the wheels, 3ft 6in diameter, were powered by cylinders 13 x 20in. The winding drum, between the frames at the rear, was driven by vertical cylinders 10 x 9in. The rope was paid out from the upper side to keep it off the ground as much as possible. A system of gearing allowed the rope to be run out without running the engine. The grate area was 6.9ft^2; heating surface: firebox 67ft^2, tubes 481ft^2, total 548ft^2. The saddle tank carried 450 gallons and the coal bunker 10cwt. The engine weighed about 22 tons in working order. The LNWR decided not to adopt the idea. A letter from Handyside Co asking the LNWR if it would purchase the permanent way materials laid down for the experiments was submitted by Footner at a meeting of the PW, Works and Estate Committee on 15 November 1876, but it was declined. Instead the 'Crewe Goods' 2-4-0s rebuilt with side tanks were found able to climb the incline with two or three wagons. So, on 16 April 1877, the Hopton stationary engine went out of use and locomotive haulage was used from Middleton top, ending the use of horses from there to Hopton foot.

The well-known photograph of the 2-4-0 tank posed on the incline with a train dates from between June 1889, when it was renumbered 3049, and June 1894 when it was scrapped. It shows the train on the 'downhill' line, and the 'uphill' line apparently out of use. A later photograph shows a 2-4-0 'Chopper' tank at the same place; the uphill line was by then much more overgrown.

The incline gradient of 1 in 14 remained the same throughout its length. In the report of the 1886 inspection it was suggested that the gradient should be eased. Nothing had been done by 21-22 June 1893 when another inspection party suggested that a plan and estimate should be prepared for easing the gradient. Still nothing was done for another 10 years until, on 12 August 1903, the Passenger Traffic Committee minuted an order from

Horses hauling wagons at the top of the Whaley incline in 1952, shortly before closure
(R. Rawlinson, Frank Armstrong collection)

LNWR 2-4-0T 3097 at Cromford Wharf between November 1887 (when renumbered 3097) and January 1903 when sold. It probably travelled from Buxton on the MR via Matlock; not by the CHPR and two rope inclines. Note the Midland signal on the right, below the canal.
(Arthur Walker)

Interior of Sheep Pasture engine house in 1942
(H.C. Casserley)

2-4-0T 2275 at Cromford Wharf

the Engineering Department: 'In order to facilitate the working and enable heavier loads to be taken up the incline, a portion of the line at the foot of it to be raised, so as to improve the gradient – Estimated cost £440.'

The embankment at the incline foot was raised and extended to give gradients from the bottom of 1 in 60 for 200yd, 1 in 30 for 75yd, and 1 in 20 for 100yd, leaving only 200yd of 1 in 14 near the top where the gradient was again eased to 1 in 470. By this time the disused uphill line had been removed. The gradient posts did not correspond to the gradient changes.

The 1886 report also recommended that the old engine and other machinery at Hopton top was to be taken down and sent to Crewe. The engine house was to be left standing for possible conversion to a cottage for an employee, but this was not done. The engine was still in place in 1892, for in the Officers' Committee minutes on 15 March the attention of Stevenson and Webb was drawn to the question of the removal of the stationary engines at Shallcross top, Bunsall top and Hopton top. Attention was drawn to the delay in supplying engines with water at Hopton top. Webb was asked to consider the best means of effecting an improvement. Another recommendation was a loop 260yd long at the top of the Hurdlow deviation. The formation was already made for the rails.

By 1883 Sheep Pasture engine was worn out. It was replaced on 10 February 1884 by a two-cylinder horizontal engine converted from the chassis of a Ramsbottom DX class 0-6-0. Cylinders 17 x 24in received steam at 80psi from an old DX boiler. The drive was through bevel gearing onto the former crankshaft.

Around 1897-98 the then new Webb 0-4-2 Bissell-truck saddle tanks were tried on the line, but insufficient water capacity led to their replacement by the Webb 'Chopper' 2-4-0 side tanks, built in 1886-87 and 1884-85. Of the original 50 all but 10 were rebuilt as 2-4-2 tanks. The 10 2-4-0 tanks became LMS 6420-9. They handled most of the CHPR traffic until the late 1920s. Withdrawals led to the return of the 0-4-2STs and 7856/8/9/61/9 were used for short trips in the 1930s. The last of the 2-4-0Ts, 6428, as BR 58092, was withdrawn from the Sheep Pasture top section in 1952.

In 1930 the LMS began transferring former North London Railway outside-cylinder 0-6-0 side tanks to the CHPR. Ten of these worked on the line. One, 27521, was involved in the derailment at the foot of Hopton incline on 6 October 1937 (see p70), after which it was withdrawn. The last, BR 58850 (formerly LMS 27505) was withdrawn from the CHPR in September 1960. It is now preserved on the Bluebell Railway.

The use of the NLR tanks was partly a result of the transfer of Cromford and Middleton sheds from being sub-sheds of Buxton, with its link via Longsight to Crewe, to Rowsley with its link to Derby. This led to the transfer of LMS Kitson 0-4-0 saddle tank No 7000 from the brewery network at Burton on Trent to the Sheep Pasture top section about 1940. The strangest visitor was former Caledonian 0-4-0ST 56020, also from Burton on Trent, to the High Peak Junction section in 1952. it was later removed to Bromsgrove from where it was withdrawn in 1955.

The Kitson tank, then 47000, derailed and overturned into a garden at Steeplehouse on 30 July 1955 (see p71) and was replaced by ex MR 0-4-0 side tank 41536, again from Burton on Trent, until 47000 was returned from Derby on 10 December after repair. For short periods in the 1960s 47000 was joined by BR Horwich built 0-4-0STs 47007 and 47006 which also worked the High Peak Junction section until they were replaced by class 03 diesels, at Cromford on 26 April 1965 and at Sheep Pasture top on 14 September 1966. At the latter the diesel, 2383, had been on load tests since 8 August.

On 7 April 1959 350hp diesel-electric 0-6-0 12006 was tried from Parsley Hay to Middleton top. After an uneasy passage of Gotham curve it reached Middleton top, but disgraced itself on the return by only just managing to crawl up Hopton incline on its own, at walking pace. Also its inability to run at over 15mph was a disadvantage.

After withdrawal of the NLR 0-6-0Ts traffic on the Middleton top – Parsley Hay section was worked by ex War Department Austerity 0-6-0 inside-cylinder saddle tanks, LNER class J94. First to arrive was 68030 on 10 April 1956. After successful trials it was followed in August by 68006 and 68013; and by 68012/68/79 in 1959-62. The J94s, also used widely by the National Coal Board, proved the ideal locomotive on the CHPR, with their short wheelbase of 11ft, tractive effort of 23,879lb and free-steaming boiler. Nos 68006/12 worked the last train, a Stephenson Locomotive Society special, on Sunday 30 April 1967, a week after the line was officially closed to traffic.

NOTES

1. Much of the information on the locomotives was obtained from notes in the Journal of the Stephenson Locomotive Society August 1951, pp 205-10, from a paper presented by G. A. Aston on 17 February 1951.
2. *The Vulcan Foundry Locomotive Works 1830-1930* pub 1930.
3. SLS Journal November 1951 p 292.
4. The spelling 'break' and 'brake' were both equally used in the mid 19th century.
5. *The Glossop Record* 9 January 1864.
6. Desbrière. Address to La Société de Ingénieurs Civils 18 March 1863.
7. Tyler. Minutes of Proceedings, Institution of Civil Engineers, Vol. 26, 1866-87, p 313.
8. PRO RAIL 410/243
9. *The Locomotive Magazine* 15 July 1933 pp 206-08.

2-4-0T, LMS 26428, and LNWR signal, Cromford Wharf, August 1940
(John Marshall)

2-4-0T 6428 at Sheep Pasture top 1942
(H.C. Casserley)

NLR 0-6-0T, LMS 27530, at Cromford Wharf, June 1941. The water tank, filled from a spring, supplied the tank wagons. Former CHPR Agent's house above
(John Marshall)

Webb 0-4-2ST 7859 at Cromford shed, 29 August 1935 *(W.A. Camwell)*

NLR 0-6-0T 58860 ascending Hopton incline with two water tanks, 5 June 1950 *(W.A. Camwell)*

Stationary boiler at the back of Middleton loco shed. Mounted on a water tank chassis, this boiler from an ex LNWR locomotive latterly supplied steam for the incline *(John Holroyd)*

The interior of Middleton winding house. *(D.W.K. Jones)*

Kitson 0-4-0ST 47000 at Sheep Pasture top, 29 July 1956 *(W.A. Camwell)*

5. Permanent Way and Formation

The use of locomotives made it necessary to replace the cast-iron rails by wrought-iron. The reason was clear enough: with cast-iron rails in 4ft lengths curves were a series of straights at obtuse angles. Wheels would strike the outside rails and exert a horizontal load. With light wagons pulled by horses the rails could withstand this, but locomotives of much greater weight moving at higher speed exerted too great a load and the rails would break. Replacement of the cast-iron rails began in 1843, at first using rails 15ft long in chairs on the original stone blocks. About six miles between Ladmanlow and Whaley Bridge were laid with wrought-iron bridge-section (⎍) rails weighing 45lb/yd on longitudinal sleepers, but this was not satisfactory. Later transverse wooden sleepers were used at 3ft 9in centres.

Cast-iron rails were still being obtained, however, and there is no doubt that prompt delivery was expected. In a letter dated 13 September 1851 Barton reminded Peter Brown at Butterley that rails ordered a month ago had still not been delivered and that others had been sent to David Wheatcroft at his limestone quarry (probably Hopton) but that as he had not ordered them they had been sent on to the CHPR. At the meeting of CHPR directors on 8 August 1855 Captain Moorsom stressed the importance of replacing the permanent way and he insisted that the traffic would not be carried satisfactorily until the cast-iron rails had been replaced by wrought-iron. He feared the directors had allowed the most favourable time for purchase of wrought-iron rails to pass by and he left it with the company to decide, but he stressed its urgency. The total estimate, including 5 per cent for himself, was £16,346.

At the directors' meeting at Cromford on 21 August 1855 he presented tenders including one from the GWR Co for best selected old rails to be delivered at Bull Bridge (where the North Midland line passed under the Cromford Canal) at £5 10s 0d per ton. He was authorized to purchase up to 1,000 tons from the GWR. On 13 September 1855 the CHPR committee accepted Moorsom's estimates and agreed to his terms, at the rate of 5 per cent of the cost of the works, and it was agreed to engage him as engineer for this work.

Rails were mostly obtained second-hand from the Midland and LNWR companies. On 12 October 1855 a Midland tender was accepted for double-headed rails at £7 a ton and single-headed rails at £7 5s a ton. (There would, of course, be a greater length of single-headed rails for the same weight). A further order for 600 tons of iron rails at £7 15s a ton was given to Begbie & Co on 30 April 1856, 'to be delivered ex ship at Liverpool.' On 11 June 1856 Francis Barton confirmed a contract for larch sleepers at 1s 2½d and 1s 3d a foot and on 31 July it was reported that the company had contracted to purchase rails to relay the line between Buxton (Ladmanlow) and Whaley Bridge, and that the works on that section were progressing. The junction with the SD&WB was not yet begun, but plans were prepared and it was staked out.

On 28 November 1856 Broome, on behalf of the Buxton Lime Co, requested the use of old rails for the proposed branch to the Grin lime kilns. It was agreed that 1600yd of rails for a single line of that length were to be lent to the Buxton Lime Co. At the same time an order was to be given to William Bird & Co for 120 tons of rails to be delivered at Gloucester at £7 15s 0d a ton. Barton was authorized on 26 March 1857 to purchase sufficient sleepers to complete the line from Whaley Bridge to the bottom of the Shallcross incline. Blenkinsop reported on 11 April that relaying between Whaley Bridge and Buxton was in progress, and that the inclines were being overhauled ready for the opening of the junction with the SD&WB. This must have included construction of a new embankment to ease a sharp curve just north of Buxton tunnel, because the old embankment still carries some of the original stone blocks with the imprint of the cast-iron rails. Rule 53 in the 1858 Rule Book limited speed on wrought-iron rails to 12mph and on cast-iron rails to 5mph.

For relaying the line between Sheep Pasture and Middleton inclines instructions were given on 27 January 1860 for 70 tons of wrought-iron rails 50lb/yd to be obtained. The 70 tons would make only 3136 yards of rail, not enough for one mile of track. Payment was to be made out of proceeds from the sale of redundant cast-iron rails. However, on 1 March 1860 Smith reported that the Sheep Pasture length of line was so much better than he expected that its renewal should be suspended. But the railway from Harpur Hill to Ladmanlow was reported to be in a very bad state.

At the end of 1860 the company ordered '100 tons of Barlow's Patent Rails from the LNWR for the repair of the railway'. During the period of lease to the LNWR relaying continued slowly, mostly using second-hand LNWR rails. The extra cost of transverse wooden sleepers instead of the old stone blocks was reported on 16 January 1862 to be £60 a mile. Although an order was given to use sleepers, many lengths continued to be laid in chairs on the old stone blocks.

On 17 November 1864 Smith's recommendation to replace stone blocks by transverse sleepers on sharp curves was considered. He explained that with increased traffic it was difficult to maintain the track to gauge. The order was given to replace the blocks, at an estimated cost of £427. In March 1863 it was reported that there were still about 9 or 10 miles laid with cast-iron rails, and that these were breaking at the rate of about 700 a month. Smith stated that the estimated cost of relaying the road with second-hand wrought-iron rails including creosoted sleepers but allowing for cast-iron rails to be removed, was £650 per mile. Smith's report was ordered to be referred to John Ramsbottom who was to be asked if he could provide lighter engines

Coaling J94 68006, one lump at a time, at Middleton top, 30 April 1967 *(T.A. Fletcher)*

NLR 0-6-0T 58856 on SLS/MLS tour rounding Gotham Curve, 27 June 1953 *(W.A. Camwell)*

Cast-iron bridge at Longcliffe, GR 225557, as renewed in 1865, 26 February 1978 *(John Marshall)*

to reduce the rate of breakage so that the rails might continue in use until worn out, and if he could give his opinion on the most desirable and economical course to be taken. Smith also reported that about 300 chairs of the wrong pattern were put down in the relaying of the Minninglow length in 1862 as a temporary arrangement but they were still in place and should be replaced without delay. A letter dated 16 April 1863 to the Permanent Way Committee recommended the relaying of the remaining 9½ miles of cast-iron rails (but not the inclines) with old light-section LNWR rails with chairs on the existing stone blocks. The tender of John Pickering at 1s per lineal yard was accepted for the relaying on 7 August 1863. Another report from Smith on 17 September urged the relaying of Sheep Pasture, Middleton and Hopton inclines with wrought-iron rails at an estimated cost of £1,032 10s 1d. This was accepted and the work was to be carried out by Pickering. Bearing in mind that the 'existing stone blocks' had only one hole in each filled with an oak plug for a single spike, the attachment of chairs involving making one or two more holes in each block must have been laborious unless only one spike was used per chair. Not all the relayed track was proving ideal. There had been much botching with poor quality second-hand material. Smith reported on 5 February 1864 that a portion of the main line between the junction with the SD&WB and Shallcross incline, on which there was considerable traffic in marshalling trains and shunting, was too weak and was difficult to keep in order and was expensive in maintenance. He recommended that it should be relayed with the type of rail used on the SD&WB, at an estimate of £540 7s 9d after deducting the value of old materials. It was ordered that the line should be renewed. But the botching went on. On 19 May 1864 Smith was authorized to take up a further half mile of usable bridge rails between Ladmanlow and Whaley Bridge for repairing other portions of the line. Payment to John Pickering of £157 for relaying was ordered on 16 June.

Difficulty in keeping track to gauge where it was laid on the original stone blocks on curves was reported by Smith on 17 November, and he recommended substitution of transverse sleepers. His estimate of £427 was approved and the work was carried out. On 21 September 1865 he was ordered to take up another mile of the bridge rail between Ladmanlow and Whaley Bridge and to relay with old LNWR rails and to use the bridge rails for repairs as mentioned above. Smith was pushing ahead with the relaying but it was painfully slow. On 21 February 1866 he was asked to submit a diagram showing the portion of the line that had been laid with wrought-iron rails and the portion he intended to relay in that year. He was asked to do no more than was absolutely necessary, *bearing in mind the proposed conversion of the line into a passenger railway.* No such proposal has been found. It seems strange, considering that the 'fly' service was still in operation and, as mentioned in Chapter 7, its withdrawal was being discussed. At last, on 18 February 1867, Smith was able to report that the only remaining cast-iron rails were in sidings.

Even at this date portions were still laid with the light bridge rails. On 14 March 1867 Smith was authorized to take up another mile of these 'between Buxton and Whaley Bridge' for repairing other portions of the line with similar rails, and to replace them with standard rails. There were still about 7¼ miles of bridge rails in April 1869, but their total replacement could not have been delayed long after that. A few of the cast-iron fish-bellied rails remain today at the inspection pit in the workshop at Cromford. (See photograph p10)

After 30 years the four iron under-bridges were suffering from the heavy traffic. Smith reported on the bridge over the Goyt at the foot of the Whaley incline on 17 November 1862 and its reconstruction at an estimated cost of £206 was recommended. According to Warren's diary this was done on 1 May 1863. The woodwork was replaced but not the cast iron. The bowstring girders, which are still in existence, were erected later. (See photograph p52)

On 18 June 1863 Smith explained the need for a plan of the CHPR and he stated that he had had an offer from a local surveyor to carry this out for £60. He was authorized to negotiate with the surveyor for a complete plan to a scale of 2 chains to 1 inch (1:1584) showing the whole line and works including adjoining surplus lands. The plan was to be uniform with those prepared under Frederick Wood, the LNWR land agent.

Smith issued a warning on 17 November 1864 that the three iron skew bridges over roads needed renewing because the original girders had fractured. Two, on the Middleton incline and at Longcliffe, were renewed with cast-iron girders by Smedley Bros of Belper to whom the contract, at £5 15s per ton for 26 tons of ironwork, was awarded on 16 March 1865. The third bridge, over the new Macclesfield road at Ladmanlow, was renewed with wrought-iron girders by E. Taylor of Swanwick, Derbyshire, whose tender, for £14 per ton, was accepted on 20 April 1865. On 15 January 1866 the PW Works and Estate Committee ordered Smith to take down and rebuild the wing wall at the south-east corner of the bridge carrying the Cromford – Belper turnpike road (now the A6) over the foot of the incline at Cromford, at an estimated cost of £32.

At a spot near Whaley Bridge where, because of sharp curves and shunting of heavy mineral trains, it was difficult to keep the track in proper order, Smith was authorized, on 17 October 1867, to lay down six pairs of 21ft steel rails. These were the first steel rails on the CHPR, though they had been in use on the LNWR since 1862.

It was reported on 23 September 1869 that an inspection of the CHPR had revealed that all was in good order except about ¾ mile near Hurdlow and another stretch near Newhaven tunnel, apparently from long neglect. Smith threatened the gangers on these lengths with dismissal if the track was not put in good repair immediately. Although no part of the line required relaying at that time, he suggested that when Buxton tunnel required relaying the committee should consider whether new rails might best be used, instead of selected old rails as elsewhere.

The abandonment of stationary engine working on Whaley Bridge incline, referred to on p39, was only the beginning of over 20 years of mining subsidence in the Whaley Bridge and Shallcross areas, despite Section 14 of the CHPR Act of 1825 which ruled 'No mine to be worked to the prejudice of the Railway'. On 23 May 1876 Joseph Cooksey & Sons, mining engineers of West Bromwich, and mining consultants for the LNWR, wrote to Harry Footner, superintendent of the CHPR section from February 1876, to explain that the Shallcross Colliery Company's workings were then under the engine house and reservoir.

Correspondence on the matter continued for about ten years. On 4 March 1885 Joseph Cooksey & Sons wrote to L. & E. Hall of the Shallcross Mining Co notifying them of the expense incurred in repairing and restoring the track and reservoir on the Shallcross incline, and stating that this should be repaid to the railway company. The work up to 1884 had involved 83 wagons of ash and ballast costing, with labour, £25 16s 10d; raising the reservoir bank £14 14s 0d; and pipes £2 7s 3d. On 18 March 1885 Footner was able to report that the matter had been decided in favour of the railway company.

In July 1886 Mr Jodrell of the Whaley Bridge colliery gave notice to the company through Cooksey that he intended to work coal under the line, warehouse and engine shed at Whaley Bridge. Cooksey & Sons were asked to negotiate for the purchase of two plots of coal at an estimated cost of £800. On 13 October it was reported that he had agreed for the purchase of a total of 9,727yd^3 of coal for £672 1s 3d, plus the agent's fee of £22.

Whaley incline from bridge over River Goyt, October 1950 *(E.R. Morten)*

6. Interlude: A Journey Over the High Peak Railway

'Crewe Goods' on Gotham curve between February 1887, when it was numbered 3083, and June 1892 when it was withdrawn.

'No poetry in railways!' foolish thought
Oh a dull brain, to no fine music wrought.

These opening lines of *Railways* by Charles Mackay (1846) preface Chapter 24 of *All About Derbyshire* by Edward Bradbury, published by Simpkin Marshall & Co. in 1884, in which he describes a footplate journey over the CHPR from Shallcross to Cromford on 10 July 1880. The account, more than any other contemporary document, brings the CHPR to life and, what is more, it describes a journey over the long-abandoned section from Shallcross to Ladmanlow. With the omission of several unnecessary florid passages the chapter is reproduced here:–

Most tourists in Derbyshire have encountered, at some point or another, the acute curves, and sensational gradients of the Cromford and High Peak Railway . . . This morning I am to traverse the whole extent of the line on the engine, or rather engines, for the railway is divided for working purposes into eight sections . . . Like all single lines, the traffic is worked by what in railway parlance is known as the "staff system". The staff is a truncheon painted and lettered specially for the division of line over which it acts as the *open sesamé.* It is suspended on the weatherboard of the engine, and no train or engine may enter any section without being in possession of the engine staff belonging to that section. The driver cannot start without this staff, which he receives from the official in charge of the staff station; and on arriving at the station to which the staff extends, the talisman is given up to the person conducting that place. Through or local, "up" or "down", "fly" or "slow", there are twenty-two trains a day on the High Peak Railway, and the fastest trains occupy a space of over five hours in performing the entire journey.

I am at Whaley Bridge this July morning; and before half the world has breakfasted, and while housemaids, drowsy and slovenly, are yawningly lighting the fire to prepare the matutinal meal, the through "up" train to Whatstandwell is off and away. Due out at ten minutes past seven o'clock, we are timed to arrive at the Cromford terminus at a quarter past twelve, according to the current timetable, which is dated "December, 1876, and until further notice"; an arrangement which is primitive and simple, and makes one wish that the hours of departure and arrival of all trains in "Bradshaw" savoured equally of the unvarying constancy of the Medes and the Persians. One leaves Whaley Bridge with its factories and colliery gins and slag heaps, without regret. The first mile or so of the ride is achieved in the guard's brake, and is up the Shallcross gradient, a straight rise of 1 in $8^1/_2$. The line here is double, and is worked by an endless chain (Shallcross incline had a wire rope from 27 February 1868). Presently we are among the bold features of the Derbyshire moorland hills; and the Goyt on our right is running innocently away between the banks of lichened rock, coy fern, and hanging trees. A locomotive meets us at the summit of the line, and working tender first, is taking on our train of some twenty waggons; a cargo which is a curious *olla podriga* of grains, barrels of beer, bags of beans, sewing machines, flour, lime, coal, cans of paint, boxes of tea, and agricultural implements. To one accustomed to the swift, smooth, motionless motion of a Pullman palace car, or a Midland bogie carriage, the jerking, jolting, jig-dancing of the engine of the High Peak Railway is an experience to remember as a certain specific for the cure of indigestion. The seven o'clock breakfast is already shaken down; and no wonder that Toodles, the stoker, is feeding himself as well as the engine. Toodles is a grotesque combination of grit and grease, and might have been carved out of a column of coal and then roughly oiled and toned down; while his "mate", the driver, an older man, is suggestive of an impossible partnership between a butcher and a chimney sweep, wearing – as he does – the blue blouse of the one, and the mosaic soot of the other.

We are now in full swing; and everything about the train strikes me as being mechanically malevolent, discordant, and out of temper. The engine has not the mellow "fluff, fluff", and the full-voiced, deep throated "chay-chay", of its superior locomotive brethren, the race horses of the main line. It spits its way along spitefully, and starts with a jerk, and stops with a jump, and goes with an irregular lurch throughout that is trying to one who has not acquired his "sea-legs". The waggons, through not being so closely united in the tightness of "coupling" as they might be, batter away at each other as if each individual truck had quarrelled with its partner, and was settling its grievances in blows . . .

Now the whole train seems bent on going a trip over the low stone walls into the neighbouring moors to the right; then it evinces that it has changed its mind and has a disposition for toppling over to the left. Between walls of woodbine and ivy now; then to the right, the deep wooded shade of Errwood Hall, as the line runs along a terrace of rock, high over the wild, green glen beauty of the Goyt Valley. Presently Bunsall is reached. Here the engine leaves us, and the train is pulled in instalments up the steepest gradient on the line, varying from one in seven to one in eight. It is a double one, the first straight, the second on the curve. The operation is a long and tedious one; but at last the whole train is marshalled on the summit. Another locomotive is waiting to take us on, and I am making friends with the two fresh engine men, greasier and grittier than the last, and I am learning to balance myself on another quivering foot board, as we pant through a wild, bleak, hilly country. We seem to be moving along the top of the world; there are deep hollows in the hills below; and every variety of peak and rounded knoll. The journey is a scamper across savage and solitary moors. The heather grows to the verge of the line. The rarefied air blows about you like a fresh sea breeze. The train is the only moving thing in sight, save when a wild grouse, or a curlew, rises with a sharp startled cry. Then . . . a sudden scream from the engine takes the startled air and darkness shrouds the speeding train. "Burbage Tunnel", yells Toodles in my ear, as he opens the firebox, and stands like a Salamander in a white dazzling circle of heat. But the wind has hurried away with his words. A thousand echoes are fighting with each other; the west walls fly past like a rushing river; there is a furious whirlwind of tumult, and a damp chill that might belong to the Styx. The train, indeed, might be Charon's boat; and the driver, standing so statuesque and silent in the broad, blinding circle of white light, with his eye strained in earnest watchfulness, and his hand fixed with decisive hold on the cold glistening regulator, might be Danté's infernal ferryman. In the distance, however, there is hope. A glimpse of light, looking as big as half-a-crown, widens. It grows larger, until, with a wild shriek of exultation from the snorting engine, we emerge from the confined vault, with its darkness and damp, and strange unearthly noises, into the glad blue light and freedom again, and see the windows of Buxton flashing back the sunlight far away below our breezy table-land. Half-a-mile long, the Burbage tunnel is the only one on the High Peak Railway of any importance, and it is dirty enough and wet enough for them all.

"This is Ladmanlow", ventures the driver, shutting off the steam. The information anticipates my query, for there are no name-boards on any of the stations to indicate your whereabouts. The stations, indeed, are but sheds; and they sometimes seem to be the only erections within miles of anywhere. Some time is now occupied in the operation known as "shunting", the dropping of one waggon off, and the coupling of another on; sending this truck down that siding, and fetching that truck from another. After thus playing at a species of truck-tennis with the entire train for some time, we rattle along again. Past Diamond Hill; past the stony slopes of Solomon's Temple; past Harpur Hill, with the tall, insolent, ugly, ubiquitous chimney which threatens the vision of the Buxton visitor wherever he may be, whether on the top of Corbar, or on the slopes of Axe Edge, or at the Cat and Fiddle, or at Fairfield. And now the landmarks are lost, and we are running with a rattle and a roar over the moors. The engineman treats his iron horse as if he were driving a living animal. He knows her faults and her good points. He can tell at what part of the road she wants whip and loose rein, and when he must hold her in with tight hand. And the iron Bucephalus responds as if sensitive to his will, and the slightest movement of the regulator is as a touch of spur, and makes her spring on like a creature of blood and nerves. Now a hare starts by the side of the line; now some grouse rise with noisy "'cluck-cluck"; again, a flight of crows, making for some feeding place, is the only sign of life in the lofty loneliness. here there are fields on either side of the rough track; but what the unsophisticated eye takes for sheep grazing are really so many obtruding blocks of gray limestone. Hindlow is the next stopping place. "Low" in the Peak District means "high"; and the quaint old Derbyshire people describe a residence in these exposed altitudes as "living out of doors". Hurdlow is the succeeding station ("low" again), and this is the highest point of the High Peak Line. To get here there was formerly a third incline, but the gradient has been rendered workable by locomotive. A change of guard, and transfer to a third engine, with driver and fireman who can hold their own in grease and grit with their ebony colleagues. There is no water supply at this *depôt*, and to assuage the Iron Horse's thirst, water is brought in large tanks from Ladmanlow. More truck tennis; and then we bump along again; now upon a terrace of rocky embankment; now in a steep cutting, with the naked limestone rocks clothed in flounces of green which you can gather as you pass, so scanty is the clearing; now a sharp whistle of warning from the engine to announce our approach to some platelayers, who leap aside with pick and shovel just in time as we whisk past in a cloud of steam. Anon we rush under a bridge carrying a road that seems to lead nowhere; then we pause at a little one-horse kind of station called Parsley Hay, which looks just like a wayside shed on an American prairie line. The guard seems to combine the duties of station-master, shunter, clerk, signalman, porter, and inspector. Indeed, he seems to be the only element of existence about the place . . .

Between Friden and Minninglow is the great Gotham Curve . . . and then we stop at Bloore's siding. Who is Bloore that he should have a siding? He is evidently a man of bricks. But the subject is not one that is likely to throw the world into convulsions of controversy; and the engine is panting away again. The scenery, truth to tell, has not been specially attractive during the last few miles . . . Rather a monotonous table-land, where niggard fields and stubborn heath are ruled off with bleak stone walls, and the perspective is unbroken save here and there by a clump of storm-rent ragged pines. At Longcliffe, however, the views are more diversified; and we get in a pleasant country of hill and dale, with glimpses of wood and water, rendered all the more pleasing to the artistic eye by the sudden lighting up of the picture by the sun, which has been sulking behind gray clouds all day. As Hopton is approached there is some bold rock scenery; and the limestone cuttings show engineering works of great difficulty. Another engine is harnessed to ours here, and with both brakes screwed down, we slide down the incline to Middleton.

Picturesque enough to make me wish to enchant hither the painters by whom it would be most appreciated is the view now, with the Black Rocks pointing over the Matlock Valley, and Barrel Edge rising in serried ranks of pine and fir above them, and the filmy smoke of peaceful Wirksworth rising lazily from the green-wooded hollow beyond. That sleepy hollow is Adam Bede's country . . .

But there is something else to think about besides George Eliot. There is the Middleton incline to go down. The locomotive leaves us; and down below drops the shining track of steel, its diminishing lines a study of perspective. The gradient is 1 in 8½, and the train is let down two waggons at a time by a coiled wire rope from a stationary engine. *(Middleton incline was single-line at this period).* You must be quite prepared to hazard the risk of the run down. Sometimes a waggon *does* break loose, and it will not stop to be reasoned with, but goes to swift destruction. Ride across the buffer, and be prepared to jump off at once if anything gives way. The hook is coupled to the waggons. Off we glide. The cable swings and clangs ominously as it strikes the steel rollers, which seem to say "Caution!" in a metallic voice that keeps repeating itself all the way down. Steeplehouse is the next station; and here *the* view of the line is beheld as, riding on yet another locomotive, we pass directly under the Black Rocks and see through the green veil of the sunlit woods that vision of Matlock, with the deep crags of the Derwent valley, which is like a piece of sublime theatrical scene-painting from a romantic opera. There is another of those creepy, dithery inclines at Sheep Pasture, with a gradient on the curve of 1 in 8 down to Cromford, but one forgets the risk of riding on buffers, in the green beauty of the scene, for the rocky cutting through which the line winds is a fern paradise that is a revelation of loveliness.

Another locomotive to take the train to High Peak Junction at Whatstandwell. The unique "Oozly bird" came over to this country, it is well known, in two ships; but to get over the High Peak Line involves at least half a dozen locomotives. No, thank you very much, Toodles. I will not ride down to the Junction. My bones have been sufficiently dissected; and "The Greyhound" at Cromford is eloquent of a refreshing bath, and of a well cooked dish of plump trout that were rising at flies in the cool Derwent an hour ago.

7. Further developments under the LNWR

Crewe Goods 2-4-0 at top of Hurdlow deviation between 1887 when it was renumbered 3083 and 1892 when it was withdrawn. Exact site confirmed by remains of ramp and the landscape beyond.

As might be expected on a railway in such a remote district, changes on the CHPR occurred slowly following the lease to the LNWR in 1861. William Smith continued as secretary with responsibility for engineering matters until he moved to Crewe in 1868. His name continues to appear in the minutes and it was he who signed the CHPR rules issued in 1877. It will be recalled that he also signed the previous rules of 1858. After 22 years as divisional engineer on the Crewe and Holyhead divisions, during which time he was engineer on the Ffestiniog tunnel (it was on this line that the old CHPR locomotive No.4 was used for ballasting work, see p37), Smith retired in 1889 and died at Liverpool on 12 November 1911 at the age of 86[1]. For a short period after his move to Crewe in 1868 the secretary was Edward Lacey of Burbage. Francis Barton then resumed as secretary, occupying the agent's house at Cromford.

From 1862 LNWR officials made regular inspections of the railway and reported to the Board. The inadequacies of the tiny workshop at Cromford (see photograph p58) resulted in an inspection in June 1862 by Thomas Broome, William Smith, John Ramsbottom and R. S. Norris to find an alternative site. They recommended Ladmanlow, as it was on the longest level stretch and with easy access to Longsight and Crewe. In July 1862 Charles Mason (assistant manager, LNWR) carried out an inspection and prepared a report[2] addressed to William Cawkwell, general manager, Crewe, in which he recommended the establishment of only a small maintenance shop at Ladmanlow. At Cromford eighteen men were employed in the shop and many of their children worked in Arkwright's mill at Cromford. Foundry work was carried out promptly at Derby. It was decided to leave the workshop at Cromford.

Mason noted that management of the local traffic at Whaley Bridge to and from the High Peak line continued in the hands of the Buxton Lime Co. He recommended that it should be amalgamated with the ordinary railway business at Whaley Bridge whereby the company would save from £150 to £200 a year. Also it would enable a better check to be kept on exchange of traffic with the Peak Forest Canal which was in the hands of the MS&L. There was nothing to prevent the change from taking place at once.

He noted large quantities of old iron such as disused wheels and axles, rails and wagon iron at the top of Whaley Bridge incline, Ladmanlow and at other places, and suggested that it should be removed to the company's stores and disposed of to avoid waste and pilferage. A note in the margin here states that the previous May Crewe had asked Smith not to send any more old cast-iron rails until he was ordered to do so.

Mason also commented on a road crossing at Whaley Bridge near the foot of the incline leading to a row of cottages and said that there was no right of way there, but the solicitor stated that the road could not be closed by the company. At Shallcross he noted that there was insufficient siding accommodation which resulted in excessive shunting causing needless wear and tear of engines and wagons. He remarked on six wagons loaded with cast-iron chairs bearing labels dated 16 June which had been standing around for five weeks and still with no immediate prospect of being discharged. There was an old wire rope weighing several tons rusting away on Shallcross incline; it should be removed along with the other old iron.

At Hopton he met the manager of the stone company who complained that they had lost their South Staffordshire traffic since the opening of the Severn Valley Railway. This was opened by the West Midland Railway on 1 February 1862 and became part of the GWR on 1 August 1863. The Wenlock stone was now sold in south Staffordshire at a lower price than the Hopton stone because of lower transport costs.

At a meeting on 1 April 1863[3] Smith was instructed to collect the old wire rope and other scrap material and to send it all to Longsight. Mr Kay reported that receipts on the CHPR for January 1863 were £978 5s 1d and for February £993 4s 2d. Working expenses in 1862 averaged about £870 a month but in February were £1,060.

It was at this meeting that Smith first proposed a deviation to avoid the Hurdlow incline. It stood between two levels of about 12 miles each necessitating the use of three locomotives and a stationary engine. With a deviation one locomotive and the stationary engine could be dispensed with and the line could be operated by locomotives over the 24 miles between Hopton top and Bunsall top. Smith was asked to prepare details of how it should be done and of the saving in operating costs. The deviation was considered at the meeting of the LNWR Special Committee on 17 August 1864. Smith's estimate of £7,300 for the entire work was approved on 15 September. Powers for the deviation were obtained in 1865[4]. Land purchase for the deviation was already being negotiated; Bateman's demand for £60 an acre was accepted on 18 May and £135 an acre was paid for Col. Leslie's land.

The contract for construction was awarded to George Farnsworth of Matlock for £4,211 on 20 December 1866. The engineer's estimate was £6,100. The work was delayed by acquisition of land and it was not until 14 March 1867 that Wood reported that all land for the deviation had been bought. He was told to obtain possession as early as possible and to advise Mr Smith so that work could go ahead. Work began in April 1867 and by 11 May Farnsworth had completed 2,037yd^3 of excavation and 257yd^3 of masonry and stone work, and about 250yd of walling. The estimated total of excavation was 33,100yd^3, of masonry 2,000yd^3 and 5,500yd, over 3 miles, of fence walling. The last traffic passed over the Hurdlow incline on 1 January 1869 and the single-line deviation, nearly 2 miles at 1 in 60, was opened on Monday 4 January. To facilitate working, a loop 260yd long was installed at the top in 1887.

The redundant section of original route was abandoned from 2 January and the stationary engine was removed. The incline chain, new on 18 April 1861, was transferred to Hopton incline where it was installed on 1 July 1869. About 10 acres of abandoned formation at Hurdlow and Harpur Hill were sold to the Duke of Devonshire in October 1879 for £50 which released the company from maintenance of walls. One may ask how this was justified when the Duke had given much of the land on which the railway was built.

Another important job was easing curves and cutting out contour loops. One of the biggest was at Harpur Hill where three great bends were eliminated by a shorter line, much of it in a deep rock cutting and on a high curving embankment. The contract, for £1,519, was let to Samuel Knight of Buxton on 14 March 1867. On 14 May 1868 it was reported that Smith had been given permission to borrow about 300 old 4ft cast-iron rails from the stores department to enable refuse from the Buxton Lime Company's old pits to be tipped so as to form a continuation of the Harpur Hill deviation. Permission was obtained from the Duke of Devonshire to build a solid embankment in lieu of several bridges.

It was not until 17 November 1875 that Mr Footner reported that the deviation would soon be ready for use. It had taken an extraordinarily long time to construct. Although it reduced a length of 1 mile 45 chains to 60 chains, or $^3/_4$ mile, the LNWR board decided to charge the same tolls as before.

A further problem now arose. The embankment interfered with drainage and the quick lime refuse in it poisoned surface water. In May 1879 a farmer of Harpur Hill put in a claim for £14 for a cow that had died after drinking the water. The trouble continued until April 1884 when, following a letter from the Duke of Devonshire's agent about the polluted water, it was properly drained off.

Two cottages at Longcliffe with stables beneath them were offered for sale to the railway company by the trustees of the late David Wheatcroft for £200. The matter was brought to the attention of the LNWR PW Works & Estate Committee on 16 June 1864. Smith was asked to offer £100 for the cottages, land, etc and to report to the committee. At the meeting on 16 August he read a letter declining the offer. On 17 November the trustees offered the cottages at £125, but the committee refused to go above £100. In the end, on 20 April 1865, Messrs. H. and G. Wheatcroft accepted £100. At the same meeting the committee approved an estimate of £37 for a siding at Parsley Hay.

Revenue for the railway was grabbed from whatever source presented itself. On 21 February 1866 Smith reported to the committee that thinnings from the plantations on the line were too small for railway purposes, so he had them inspected by several timber dealers one of whom offered 5 shillings for the lot. As this was the highest offer he recommended it should be accepted.

The 'fly' service continued under the LNWR, advertised only locally and not in the public timetables, at little profit to the company. Passenger receipts in 1861, the last year of separate returns,

CHPR workshop at Cromford. Billy Hallows with wooden leg, second from left, born 4 September 1836. Began as hanger-on, Sheep Pasture incline, September 1856; Middleton, 1857; 'tenting' Middleton engine July 1860; labourer in Cromford shop, 26 April 1881; transferred to incline pulley man, Cromford, 22 June 1898. Right leg injured and amputated. Returned to workshop, resigned 21 March 1904 aged 68 and died 28 October 1913. Photograph probably between 1898 and 1904.

Hurdlow station. LNWR '19in Goods' 4-6-0 entering with train, 1931. Track of Hurdlow incline, abandoned 1869, behind station

Looking down old Hurdlow incline. Site of engine house on right. 4 July 1967
(John Marshall)

were £8, collected from 121 passengers travelling at 1d a mile. During his tour of inspection in July 1862 Charles Mason met the fly train at the foot of Bunsall incline at 5.15pm. It had left Cromford at 9.00 and had taken 8¼ hours to cover 27 miles; it carried two passengers. Passenger receipts for June had been 14s 9d. Writing to Richard Moon, LNWR chairman, on 12 December 1868, Smith outlined the rules for operating the passenger traffic. Passengers paid after completion of their journeys, and the company accepted no liability for their safety. The train 'conductor' was required to look after passengers as they walked up or down the inclines. It was this that prompted Smith to ask if the passenger service could be withdrawn, or maintained only 'between Hopton and the Parks' (Harpur Hill). The LNWR Traffic Committee, however, decided that the service should continue.

At the meeting of the LNWR Special Committee on 15 January 1869 a note was read requiring the passenger carriage to be maintained and it was resolved that the surveying carriage used by Mr H. Woodhouse, PW superintendent, should be transferred to the High Peak and a new one like that of Mr Worthington, chief engineer, be built for Mr Woodhouse at a cost not exceeding £200 of which £150 should be charged to PW expenses and £50 to the carriage renewal account. By 1873 the two passenger brake vans were worn out and an order was given on 16 July for their replacement 'by two Passenger Guards Break Vans with four wheels', adding: 'Mr Bore to supply two old vans of a description suitable for the requirements of the High Peak Line'. They were ordered from duplicate stock.

With the opening of the extensions of the SD&WB and Midland railways to Buxton in 1863, and of the Midland service to Manchester in 1867, the CHPR lost its importance as a through route. The extension of the LNWR beyond Buxton to connect with the CHPR at Hindlow was already being considered. On 6 August 1866 the district goods manager at Liverpool Road station, Manchester, wrote to Richard Moon about the distance of 18 miles from Ladmanlow to Whaley Bridge via the proposed line through Buxton compared with the existing CHPR line, albeit via Bunsall and Shallcross inclines, of 7 miles. He suggested that if it proved cheaper to work traffic via the old route then it should not be abandoned. In the end, however, the cost of working the two inclines was the deciding factor.

In his report on the collision between two goods trains on 17 December 1875 when one of the firemen was killed (see p68), Captain Tyler commented that the railway had never been inspected and that it should be, in accordance with Section 77 of the CHPR Act of 1855 which ruled that a Board of Trade inspection must be carried out and a certificate obtained before passengers were carried. In view of the small number of passengers it is likely that the LNWR considered the expense of an inspection for a BoT certificate was unjustified.

At a meeting on 3 February 1876[5] the chairman stated 'that he had given orders to discontinue altogether the conveyance of passengers on the Cromford & High Peak line, and Mr Kay (district goods manager, Manchester) was instructed to write to the Buxton Lime Co. and to explain the company's inability to carry their workpeople any longer'. The service continued until the end of April 1876, and after that, apart from special trains, no more passengers were carried. The commonly repeated statement that the passenger service was terminated in 1877 following a fatal accident seems to have originated in *Our Iron Roads* by F. S. Williams (1883), and is misleading because there was no fatal accident to a passenger.

In 1875 instructions were given to convert the agent's house at Cromford into two cottages at a cost of £35. One was to be for the locomotive foreman. They were to be let at 4s a week.[6] Barton objected and stated in a letter that Mr Smith had given him an assurance that his tenancy would not be disturbed. He explained that the whole house was taken up by his work as secretary and trader on the line. However, it was of no avail and on 15 December he was ordered to vacate the house, though a reasonable time was allowed for his removal. So he had to find other accommodation near Cromford.

From 3 February 1876 Mr Harry Footner was placed in charge of the whole line and all employees[5]. By this time the main traffic was stone and lime, but a report of a runaway on the Bunsall incline on 3 October 1876 suggests that general merchandise continued to be carried. A wagon loaded with Indian corn broke away halfway up and collided with another at the bottom. Both wagons were wrecked and about 25 sacks of corn were damaged. From the wording 'halfway up' it appears the corn traffic was ascending the incline.

The first mention of full amalgamation with the LNWR occurs in the LNWR Special Committee minutes on 19 November 1875 when a letter from Mr Hubbersty, the CHPR solicitor, was read suggesting that the LNWR company should take over the CHPR absolutely, giving an equivalent of debenture stock to the shareholders in lieu of the rent then being paid. It was referred to the chairman and Mr Bancroft to consider with the solicitor and Mr Reay. The question of amalgamation was again discussed at CHPR meetings on 27 April and 26 October 1877. On 12 December the LNWR proposed to pay the CHPR Co. £100,000 in discharge of the annual payment of £4,000, but the CHPR refused to accept this. The board would accept £104,000, a sum which was declined by the LNWR.

Several matters concerning employees appear in the minutes around this period. On 16 February 1876 Footner reported that many of the 'engineers' (locomotive and stationary engine drivers) on the High Peak line had given notice to leave the railway unless their wages were increased. He persuaded the PW committee to raise their wages to £1 16s 6d

Junction of Middleton Quarry branch with C&HP at Steeplehouse.
(John Marshall)

Looking up Killers or Middleton Quarry branch near the junction with the C&HP, 1967 *(John Marshall)*

47006 Shunting in Middleton Quarry Yard, 1962.
(John Holroyd)

a week. Two had left already: driver J. Lupton and fireman G. Goodwin, jr; and two had been dismissed: driver G. Goodwin following the Turncliffe accident (see p68) and fireman H. Robinson for pushing wagons over Bunsall incline.

Various sidings were installed from time to time to cater for local traffic. An additional siding at the top of Hopton incline at a cost of £191 was approved on 15 March 1876, and on 26 April Footner was authorized to restore the connection to the Hopton Stone Quarry Company's siding at the foot of Middleton incline, at the stone company's cost. A short siding at Harpur Hill, for about four wagons, at a cost of £96, was approved on 16 August. The Buxton Lime Co. was given permission to lay down sidings there and the LNWR paid £51 for installing a connection to the main line.

The LNWR would work the lime company's wagons to the top of the lime kilns as an experiment, at one shilling a wagon. A siding connection to Briggs & Son's lime works between Hindlow and Hurdlow, which became known as Briggs Siding, was authorized on 17 October 1883 at a cost of £64 to be paid for by Briggs & Son. On 13 February 1884 an additional siding was ordered to be laid down in Shallcross yard using second-hand materials.

On 16 June 1877 the LNWR Co. set its seal on a new rule book applying to the CHPR, under the superintendence of George Findlay the chief traffic manager. It was nearly double the size of the 1858 rule book, with 84 pages plus a 3-page supplement, as against 44 pages in 1858. It comprised a section of general regulations, an enlarged section on signals, and sections devoted to station agents and staffs, flymen (or guards), engine drivers and firemen, operation of inclines, inspectors and gangers, and extracts from Acts.

In those far-off days when railways were not threatened by road competition they appeared to regard a private connection to a railway as a privilege for which the customer should pay. On 14 May 1879 Footner reported that the Hopton Wood Stone Co.'s siding leading to their Coal Hill quarry near Steeplehouse needed renewal and the junction with the main line should be relaid at once to avoid accidents. The stone company was told that it must bear the cost of the renewal of the junction if it wished to continue to use it. In the end it was agreed that the quarry company pay but only when the work was done.

On 18 May 1881 the Traffic Committee ordered weighing machines (or weighbridges) to be put down at Cromford and Ladmanlow stations at an estimated cost of £128 each. An extension to Messrs Williamson's gunpowder works siding at Fernilee, south of Shallcross top, at a cost of £57 was approved on 23 April 1884. Williamson was to pay £20 of the cost. On 14 May the Traffic Committee approved installation of a trap siding at the approach to Shallcross yard and a signal to work in conjunction with it, at an estimated cost of £33.

An application from Killer Bros, quarry owners at Middleton, for a siding connection was discussed by the Special Committee on 15 February 1882. Footner arranged for the connection to be laid in but it was not until after June 1884 that the 1190yd branch was completed by the LNWR at a cost of £3,700, paid by Killer Bros. No opening date has been found. It was worked by LNWR locomotives. Fortunately the 1 in 27 gradient favoured the loads. By an agreement on 22 August 1907 the branch was taken over by Hopton Wood Stone Firms, owners of the Middleton quarry, but LNWR locomotives continued to work the branch. Another important connection, Briggs Siding at Hindlow, was laid in at about the same time. Others were provided at Steeplehouse, Longcliffe, Parsley Hay and Harpur Hill.

Francis Barton, secretary of the CHPR, died in 1886. At the meeting on 5 November the directors offered sincere condolence to his family. A report from Messrs Farr, Mawby and Fletcher submitted to the LNWR board on 16 July 1886 recommended that Francis Webb, chief mechanical engineer at Crewe, should be responsible for the locomotive department and machinery, which he surely was anyway, and that Inspector Gould of Whaley Bridge who looked after the maintenance of permanent way should be transferred to the staff of Mr W. B. Worthington, who had just succeeded his father S. B. Worthington, as chief civil engineer of the northern division of the LNWR. Inspector Andrews was to be relieved of his position in charge of traffic arrangements and Mr Mawby was to take over the work.

The report of the inspection of October 1886 listed 34 items for attention. Besides the matters mentioned earlier, it was recommended that the sidings at Shallcross yard should be rearranged to form a 'gridiron' and on 17 November 1886 this was ordered to be carried out. The old single-headed rails scattered around the railway were to be collected and sent to Crewe. It was also pointed out that the Butterley Co's traffic was carried by the Midland. Mr Fewkes was asked to find if some of it could be carried by the Cromford Canal and over the CHPR, such an obviously inferior route that he could hardly have relished the inquiry, particularly as the Butterley Co probably remembered the affair of the bridge girders in July 1849 (p25).

Construction of a siding and loading bank for the sand and fireclay works of Green & Armitage at Longcliffe was authorized by the LNWR Traffic Committee on 14 March 1888. The LNWR was to lay the siding and stop block at a cost of £112 and Armitage was to build the loading bank and carry out alterations to the boundary wall. He was to be charged £1 a year for the use of the siding.

It was proposed that telephone circuits should be established between Whaley Bridge and Bunsall top, and between High Peak Junction and Middleton top. This was approved in November 1886 and the work was carried out shortly afterwards. An order to extend the Whaley Bridge – Bunsall top circuit to Ladmanlow and the High Peak Junction – Middleton top circuit to Longcliffe, also serving Hopton, was given in July 1887. By the early 1890s telephone communication was established over the whole line.

A curious mishap occurred on 14 April 1898 when a Great Central goods brake van, being drawn by a horse from Shallcross yard to the top of Whaley incline, fouled the bridge carrying the Buxton line, where clearance was only 10ft 6in. Traffic was interrupted until the bridge was repaired. How the poor horse took the jolt is not recorded. The GCR, as successor to the MS&L from 1897, owned the Peak Forest Canal. Possibly the brake van was carrying supplies.

The determined drive of the Midland Railway towards Buxton and Manchester caused the LNWR to see the CHPR as a step towards an outlet to the south via the North Staffordshire Railway at Ashbourne. The first positive move in this direction was the Buxton & High Peak Junction Railway, 5 miles 15 chains from Buxton to join the CHPR near the top of the Hurdlow deviation at Dowlow, and a link of 76 chains (just under a mile) from Hindlow to the CHPR at Harpur Hill, all authorized by the LNWR Act of 1874[7]. The engineer's estimate was £97,000. There were long delays in starting it and extensions of time were granted in the Acts of 1877, 1880 and finally in the Act of 1887 which revived the powers and also authorized the amalgamation of the CHPR with the LNWR.[8] From 1 July 1887 the affairs of the CHPR Co were wound up. Powers were also given for the abandonment of the portions of the CHPR made redundant by the new lines.

On 18 July 1888 the work was let to Naylor Bros of Denby Dale for £73,346. It involved considerable major engineering: Hogshaw Lane viaduct, 353yd long with 16 arches across the Wye valley in Buxton; Dukes Drive viaduct, 176yd long with 13 arches of 36ft span and a maximum height of 94ft 6in; and Hindlow tunnel 514yd long. It was the last contract to be taken on under G.W. Naylor, senior partner in the firm, who died on 13 September. The double-track main line and the single-track spur to Harpur Hill were opened on 27 June 1892. The section of the CHPR from Dowlow to Harpur Hill and from the old Macclesfield Road at Ladmanlow to Shallcross foot were abandoned.

Improvement of the remaining section to Parsley Hay, involving conversion to double track and the cutting of several corners, and also construction of the extension of 13½ miles from Parsley Hay to a junction with the NSR branch at Ashbourne, was authorized by the LNWR Act of 1890[9]. The joint tender of John Wilson & Sons of Lower Ince, Wigan, and Naylor Bros of Buxton, for £207,552 16s 5d was accepted on 14 June 1893. Construction was divided between the two firms. The engineer's estimate was £200,000.

The improvement works between Hurdlow and Parsley Hay were reported complete and a single line in use on 18 October 1893. Stations were built at Higher Buxton, Hindlow and Parsley Hay. On 1 June 1894 passenger trains began running to Parsley Hay, though the district could hardly have offered much traffic. Installation of a telephone circuit to Parsley Hay, at a cost of £96, was approved on 13 June. An Omnibus service connected Parsley Hay and Hartington. Though Parsley Hay as a village scarcely exists, the *Buxton Advertiser*, 2 June 1894, described it as 'an admirable centre for excursions by road to Hartington, Beresford Dale, the Manifold valley, Arbour Low, Lathkill Dale, Youlgreave, etc'.

The LNWR Bill for the 1890 Session also sought powers for a deviation of the CHPR of about 3½ miles from Harboro Farm, about midway between Longcliffe and Hopton top, to a point about 70yd east of the foot of Middleton incline. It was to pass round the hills to the south of the line, on an average gradient of 1 in 53 avoiding Hopton and Middleton inclines. The intention was to convert the CHPR into a passenger line as far as Middleton with stations at Friden, Longcliffe, Hopton, and Middleton for Wirksworth. The section of existing railway including the two inclines was to be abandoned. The estimated cost of the deviation was £45,415.

It was strongly opposed by the Hopton Wood Stone Co whose quarry and branch line, built at that company's expense, would lose their outlet. Another objection came from H.C.P. Gell of Hopton Hall, owner of the land occupied by Intake quarry at Middleton top worked by the Butterley Co, and Taylor's Bone Works at Hopton foot, who would also lose rail connections. In view of the objections it was agreed on 17 October 1890 to defer application for Parliamentary powers for the deviation and it was dropped from the bill because the preamble was not proved. Middleton incline therefore had to be retained, and to this we owe the preservation of a CHPR stationary engine at Middleton. Powers for improvements from Parsley Hay to near Harboro Farm were not exercised.

It will be recalled how Middleton incline had been altered for single-line working in 1856. At a meeting of the LNWR Officers' Committee on 15 March 1892 it was resolved to draw the attention of F. Stevenson and F. W. Webb to the abandonment of a portion of the CHPR from the bottom of Shallcross incline to a point about 300 yards north of Ladmanlow, in accordance with the 1874 Act, and to remove the stationary engines at Shallcross, Bunsall and Hopton. The last had been out of use since 1877. It was simpler to remove the engines in that order so that the parts could be transported on the railway. In the course of an inspection by a group of LNWR officers including Webb and Stevenson in July 1892 it was recommended that an additional line of rails should be laid on the Middleton incline with material removed from Bunsall or Shallcross inclines. A plan and estimate were drawn up by Stevenson and, following a further inspection on 21-

22 June 1893, an order was given to 'lay an additional line of rails to make it a balance incline, removing material from Shallcross to Middleton', at an estimated cost of £1,300, including the cost of removing permanent way materials from Shallcross incline. A photograph of Middleton incline top while still single track appears in *The Locomotive Magazine*, 15 July 1933 p207, wrongly captioned Sheep Pasture.

Track and engine were removed from Shallcross incline by December 1893. Shallcross top to Bunsall foot was taken up by February 1894. Bunsall incline track and engine were removed during May 1894 and the track from Bunsall top to about 300 yards short of Ladmanlow had gone by October 1894. The old Hopton engine was removed at the same time. At Middleton the 'uphill' line was relaid, a new 'drum wheel' was reported fixed to the engine in March 1894, and the incline was brought back into use with an endless rope 1,800yd long on 2 April 1894.[10] How much of the present Middleton engine is from Shallcross, or possibly Bunsall, probably will never be known, but what is certain is that the Middleton engine as preserved is substantially in its original form.

Ladmanlow engine shed was closed and the stock was transferred to Buxton. The stables at Ladmanlow, a relic of the old horse traction period, survived until 1935.

The Ashbourne line could have been built for £17,000 less had it left the CHPR about ½ mile north of Friden instead of at Parsley Hay, which was chosen as the point of diversion because it offered a better site for a station to serve Hartington, albeit 1½ miles up a long hill from the village. Had the Friden route been selected it might have involved destruction of Newhaven tunnel with its interesting plaques.

The extension to Ashbourne was opened on 4 August 1899 and from that time the CHPR was operated in two sections: Cromford to Parsley Hay, and Hindlow to Harpur Hill and Ladmanlow. The LNWR instituted through coaches between Buxton and London Euston via Ashbourne and then over the NSR, Midland, and joint lines, via Uttoxeter, Burton on Trent, Shackerstone and Nuneaton.

Beyond Ladmanlow Goyt colliery closed in 1902 and the branch was removed, but the CHPR track as far as the old Macclesfield Road remained for another 50 years. The engine shed at Middleton top

Middleton Quarry circa 1920

was burnt down on 30 July 1905, considerably damaging LNWR 2-4-0 tanks 2244 and 2278 which were inside. Various sidings, etc, installed by the LNWR are worth mentioning. Additional works at Harpur Hill for the accommodation of Buxton Lime Firms Ltd at a cost of £230 were approved on 16 January 1907. At Parsley Hay a siding was to be provided, at £335, paid for by the Derbyshire Silica Firebrick Co Ltd. This was approved on 13 March, and on 19 June further siding accommodation at the top of Sheep Pasture was approved, at £170. An order to extend the siding at the top of Hopton incline to hold 45 wagons, at an estimated cost of £166, was issued on 18 January 1911. At the same time instructions were given to replace the old goods shed at Shallcross yard by a new one 61ft x 27ft with an awning over the tracks, and a 5 ton crane to be installed there, removed from Winslow in Buckinghamshire, at an estimated cost of £760 for the shed and £141 for the crane. The tender of J. Rawlinson & Sons, Garston, for £722 13s 6d was accepted for the new goods shed on 19 July 1911. It was to be covered by asbestos sheathing.

On 23 July 1919 it was reported that the stone retaining wall of Sheep Pasture incline was bulging badly and buttresses were built to support it; £20 was paid for 440yd^2 of land for the buttresses.

Notes

1. Minutes of Proceedings, Institution of Civil Engineers, Vol. 187 1911-12. p332.
2. PRO RAIL 410/57
3. PRO RAIL 410/58 document 80.
4. LNWR (Additional Powers, England) Act, 5 July 1865, c 333, Section 24.
5. PRO RAIL 410/107, Special Committee minute 38208, 3 February 1876.
6. PRO RAIL 410/309, PW & Estate Committee minute 17614, 13 October 1875.
7. LNWR (England and Ireland) Act, 30 July 1874, c 159.
8. LNWR (Joint and Various Powers) Act, 12 July 1877, c 91; LNWR Act 6 August 1880, c 145; LNWR Act, 19 July 1887, c 131.
9. LNWR Act, 4 August 1890, c 154.
10. LNWR Officers' Meeting minute 35398, 17 April 1894.

Old course of CHPR south of Hindlow tunnel, 22 June 1964. New High Peak Junction line, opened 27 June 1892. The old course recrossed the LNWR this side of the tunnel and passed round the hill to the right. Reversing triangle to left of tunnel, marked by two trees. This is the viewpoint of the snow scene on page 72. *(John Marshall)*

End of track beyond Ladmanlow, 1892-1958, in June 1941. The arch carried the old Buxton - Macclesfield road. Buxton tunnel in distance. The section beyond here to Shallcross foot was abandoned when the High Peak Junction railway was opened on 27 June 1892. *(John Marshall)*

South end of Buxton tunnel, June 1941.
(John Marshall)

Just within the south end of Buxton tunnel showing reinforced lining, 16 May 1953 *(E.R. Morten)*

LNWR 2-4-0 tanks 2244 and 2278 at Middleton top after the engine shed fire on 30 July 1905

8. Accidents

Wrecked wagons in the catch pit on Sheep Pasture incline, probably after the runaway on 4 March 1903 *(F.W. Linaker)*

In its 137 years of operation the CHPR suffered numerous runaways, or runs as they were called, on the inclines. Most of these resulted in nothing worse than destruction of wagons and a good deal of clearing up, but a few were more serious. Rules for operation of the inclines seem to have been fairly slack at first. As early as 14 December 1830 nine empty wagons broke away while descending Middleton incline. Three crashed onto the Ashbourne road and the remaining six reached the bottom and went into an adjacent field.

Middleton incline became notorious. In 1831 there were five breakaways in one week and there was wreckage everywhere. On 3 October 1833 a runaway resulted in two fatalities. The report in the *Derby Mercury* on 9 October described how a train of six wagons arrived at Middleton top at about 6.15 on the Saturday evening. The first carried a load of 2 tons 6cwt, the second carried six passengers and the other four were empty.

'The engineer (according to the positive instructions of the committee) ordered the passengers to dismount and walk down the plane; they did dismount, but when the engineer went to set the chain in motion, the passengers got into the waggon again. The train had not advanced far when a link of the chain broke; the preventer of the leading waggon, instead of taking the ground in the usual way, and stopping the train, tripped for several yards, and checked the velocity which the breaking of the link threatened. This gave time for the passengers to jump out, on the attendants calling to them that the chain was broken. Four of them obeyed the warning, the others (two brothers) kept their seats. At this moment the preventer lost its groundings, and doubled under the waggon. The velocity became frightful for fifty or sixty yards, when the leading waggon was thrown off the rails and upset'.

The two men received fatal injuries when the other wagons piled on top of them.

Probably as a result of this accident the number of wagons allowed on the inclines, up or down, was limited to two. Runaways continued, but less frequently. In December 1856 the CHPR minutes recorded that the company was to repair the wagons of David Wheatcroft damaged in an accident on Middleton incline, and on 28 May 1858 wagons broken at the bottom of the incline were to be repaired and expenses charged equally to the CHPR, Hopton Wood Stone Co and William Wheatcroft. Warren recorded in his diary on 1 November 1860 that James Collier of Taxal was killed on the CHPR, but he gives no details of the accident.

Shallcross had its share of runaways too. Four were recorded in Warren's diary: on 16 July 1859 the chain broke and a new brake van which had cost £200 was smashed up together with a lime wagon. Evidently the chain was replaced by a rope at that time for, on 2 December following, he reported that the rope had broken resulting in the destruction of three wagons. Another wagon broke away at the top on 12 May 1863 and was smashed up at the bottom, and on 25 March 1864 five wagons belonging to the Buxton Lime Co were destroyed when they broke away. Yet another, on 10 November 1882, was reported in the LNWR PW & Estate Committee minutes.

Even the short Whaley Bridge incline did not escape. During the brief absence of the brakesman on 15 October 1875 while he was on duty elsewhere, someone maliciously turned the scotch block aside and started a loaded wagon down the plane, fortunately without damage. It was reported to the Traffic Committee[1] that on 2 October 1876 a trespasser was killed on the Shallcross incline. The following day a wagon loaded with Indian corn ran away from about half way up the Bunsall incline and collided with another wagon of corn at the bottom. A new wire rope had been installed on the incline on 26 September.

Interesting details of accidents caused by human failure are contained in a CHPR Staff Register from 1875[2]. A fireman, Henry Robinson, allowed wagons to run over the top of Bunsall incline and through the safety points, damaging one wagon and ten chairs, for which he was fined 4 shillings. Later, on 29 January 1876, he carelessly pushed wagons over the top of the incline and was dismissed on 1 February. An engine driver, Adam Dawson, was frequently in trouble. Born on 3 February 1842, he began working on the CHPR in August 1859. In 1876 he was guilty of 'careless management of his engine when approaching the top of Cromford incline' and also for 'neglecting to have steam up in his engine at the proper time at Sheep Pasture for the first train on 14 November 1876'. On 3 October 1878 he pushed a train in at Sheep Pasture top causing three wagons to run over. They derailed at the safety points just below the top. The following month, on 26 November, he ran his engine too far in Steeplehouse siding and derailed it. Another, John Sims, born on 24 May 1859, who started work as a labourer in Cromford workshop on his 23rd birthday in 1882, became a 'hanger on' at Sheep Pasture top on 11 October 1883, but not for long. He was discharged on 16 August 1884 for fastening up the safety points and leaving the stop blocks open and allowing a wagon of limestone to run down the incline.

Samuel Hallows, born 2 July 1845, began 'tenting' Hopton engine on 20 December 1875, only 16 months before it went out of use. On 26 April 1881 he began at the Middleton engine, while the incline was still single track. On 13 October 1891 he was suspended for seven days for over-winding a load of timber. On 11 June 1895, after the incline had been reconstructed with double track and the engine had been rebuilt, he was suspended for six days, from 11 June 1895, for 'over balancing' a water tank. He must have misjudged the weight of the descending wagons. He was in trouble again in 1906 when he was suspended for two days, 7-9 May, for neglecting the signal and allowing wagons to run to the bottom of the incline. It is remarkable that he remained in the company's employment until he resigned on 5 November 1913 at the age of 68.

Driver William Bradley was in trouble on 20 February 1877 for omitting to couple wagons to the engine at Middleton top, so allowing four wagons to run over the top and through the safety points. A month later, on 18 March, he derailed wagons at the bottom of Hopton incline by neglecting to hold the points to the siding. Then, on 14 June, he was late and failed to have his engine steamed up for the first train. In fact, he was not on duty until time to act as guard on the second train. James Evans, stationary engineman at Sheep Pasture, born on 29 May 1822, started work on the railway in 1839. He was accused of 'violent working of the signal from the engine house' and for drawing wagons too fast over the top on 10 February 1879 when a link broke in the tail chain and the wagons ran back and were derailed at the safety points. However, he remained on the railway until he retired in 1898 at the age of 76.

Most runaways were caused by failure of the tackling chains attaching wagons to the rope. Chain breakage caused a descending wagon of the Hopton Wood Stone Co, loaded with limestone, to break loose on Sheep Pasture incline on 31 March 1884. At the bottom it wrecked another wagon of the same firm and also damaged four others, a Midland wagon, an LNWR locomotive and the roof and a window of the workshop.

The most spectacular runaway occurred on 1 March 1888, also on Sheep Pasture, fortunately without injury or loss of life. A full report appeared in the *Sheffield Telegraph*, Saturday 3 March, and in the *Derbyshire Times*, 10 March. At about 19.00, after dark, a wagon full of lime and a brake van

Catch pit, pointsman and gong, Sheep Pasture incline (from an old sepia postcard)

loaded with about 2cwt of gunpowder in boxes cased in iron were just beginning the descent when the connecting chain broke. As the vehicles shot forward the guard and a labourer jumped off the van and landed in deep snow, which probably saved their lives. At the bottom of the incline the vehicles had reached a speed calculated at about 120mph. They leapt off the rails at the curve, flew straight over the canal, damaging its banks, and bounced over a stone wall. One of the canisters of gunpowder exploded and fragments of the vans were scattered around. In a third leap the remains of the vehicles crossed the Midland line, damaging the rails.

Mr Walker, the LNWR goods agent, and Henry Roper, foreman at Cromford, were immediately on the scene, and message was sent to the Midland signalman to stop all traffic, because a train was due. The outcome of this accident was the installation of a catch pit on the incline, just above the road bridge. Powers to acquire the additional land were obtained in the LNWR Act of 1889[3], and the catch pit was reported finished on 15 January 1890.

The incline rails ran straight down into the catch pit and the running lines passed on each side. Points above were normally set for the catch pit; on the ascending line they were weighted; on the descending line they were controlled by a pointsman in a cabin. By means of gongs placed higher up he was able to judge the speed of descending wagons. If he decided that the wagons were under control he would pull over the points to take them round the catch pit. If he judged the speed to be too great he would leave the points set for the catch pit and make a hasty retreat to a safe distance. On 10 April 1890 installation of electric bell communication between the pointsman's cabin and the engine house was approved at a cost of £13. The catch pit was certainly effective as shown in the photograph, believed to be of a runaway at 8.30 on 4 March 1903. Following this the catch pit was provided with a roof. At 15.45 on 20 May 1916 five wagons ran 1,120 yards down the incline and piled up in the catch pit, damaging the roof.

The catch pit was unable to stop a runaway on 29 May 1956. A loaded wagon was being lowered on its own, unbalanced. Just as it was passing the catch pit, at 13.00, the fastening strap broke, the chain came away from the rope, and the wagon crashed into other wagons at the bottom. There were no injuries. Apparently a catch pit was also installed near the foot of the Bunsall incline, probably about the same time. It is referred to in the LNWR 'Rules and Regulations applying to the Cromford & High Peak Section' dated April 1891. No other reference to it has been found, but as the Bunsall incline was closed in 1892 this is hardly surprising.

Two examples from the Staff Register make it appear that minor accidents must have been frequent. Driver Samuel Slack, born on 1 April 1854 and who began work on 9 September 1873, went too fast round Bank's Curve, between Hindlow and Parsley Hay, on 6 July 1878 and derailed his engine

A water tank and a flat wagon approach the foot of Sheep Pasture incline. *(D.W.K. Jones)*

and nine wagons. Exactly a week later he crashed into a horse and cart at the level crossing at Bloore's Siding when driving the 'fly' train from Hopton to Hindlow. The horse was killed and the cart was smashed up. By then the passenger service had finished, but the term 'fly train' was still used for through goods trains. Samuel Sheldon who began in 1864 and became a driver between Hopton and Parsley Hay in 1875, was discharged on 19 November 1877 for crashing through the gates at Newhaven crossing.

Collisions between trains were fortunately not so frequent. The worst was on 17 December 1875 at Turncliffe between Harpur Hill and Ladmanlow. Two goods trains collided head-on, killing one fireman and injuring the other and both drivers. Captain Tyler, in his report, commented on the unusual working arrangements. A rule in the timetable of April 1874, then in force, stated: *'The line between Ladmanlow and Harpur Hill must be worked by an Engine Staff lettered L&HH. All engines passing between these points must carry the Staff, with the Exception of the 5.00am and 10.55am trains from Ladmanlow, and the 10.15am and 3.15pm trains from Harpur Hill.*

The Enginemen in charge of these four trains must

Bridge carrying the A6 road just above the foot of Sheep Pasture incline. The original skew stone arch was widened at an unknown date by the girders seen on the near (east) side.
(W.A. Camwell)

see the Staff at the Starting Points immediately before proceeding on their Journey'.

One driver, George Goodwin, had failed to obey this rule. He was dismissed on 27 January 1876 'for a deliberate falsehood before Colonel Yolland at the Government inquiry'[14]. Goodwin had begun as a cleaner at Ladmanlow in May 1859, became a fireman on 1 March 1861 and began driving from Ladmanlow on 1 March 1862. George William Goodwin, probably his son, who began as a fireman at Ladmanlow on 26 October 1875, resigned on the day George was dismissed, on the grounds that the hours of duty were too long. He was probably right; this may have had some bearing on the accident.

An account for £1 8s 7d received from Buxton Lime Co for expenses in the burial of George Pennington, the fireman killed in the accident, was ordered to be paid on 15 March 1876, The other driver, William Chappell, born on 18 April 1837, began as a fireman in May 1858 and as a driver between Hopton and Hindlow in October 1859. In June 1862 he had begun driving from Ladmanlow. Following the collision, in which he suffered injury, he was suspended until 21 February 1876 when he resumed driving on the Ladmanlow – Bunsall – Harpur Hill sections. After breaking down the Hindlow warehouse he was in collision at Harpur Hill with a train driven by Joseph Mellor on 15 February 1877, when several wagons were damaged. Both drivers were reprimanded. Mellor had already been in trouble exactly a year before when he crashed his engine into Ladmanlow shed, breaking a door and knocking a side wall down. On 3 May 1877 he pushed some wagons too fast at the top of Bunsall incline and one went over and was derailed at the safety points.

An accident, fortunately without personal injury, at the Butterley Company's siding at Intake Quarry, Middleton top, revealed an unsafe working practice. On 10 October 1878 the fly train was passing the siding at the right time when two loaded wagons of the Butterley Co ran into the brake van, damaging the side but not derailing it. Footner stated that there were trap points in the siding but that the Butterley Co failed to keep them set properly. He ordered a throw-off switch with lock to be installed on the railway company's side of the boundary at the expense of the Butterley Co, and the key to be kept by the engine driver whose duty it was to attend to the traffic to and from the quarry. Damage to the brake van was to be paid for by the Butterley Co which, however, declined to pay for the catch points.

Derailments were frequent, though most were not serious. On 29 June 1910 a wagon in a goods train left the rails near the foot of Hopton incline and was dragged along for about ¼ mile. (There is no note of which way the train was going.) The check rail of a crossing was torn out and about 200 yards of track was damaged and 400 chairs were broken. In a similar incident at Friden on 10 August 1915 a milk van was derailed on a curve and was dragged 194 yards before the train was stopped. About 192 chairs and 50 fastenings were broken. That the single line was blocked for only about two hours suggests the PW gang was highly efficient.

A derailment which proved fatal happened near the foot of Hopton incline on 6 October 1937 when ex NLR 0-6-0T 27521, with four loaded wagons and a brake van, derailed at 45mph on the 20-chain curve while working up speed to climb the incline. It rolled down the 25ft embankment killing the driver. The engine was dismantled and taken to Derby for examination before being scrapped. Three wagons and the brake van also fell down the embankment.

The accident was investigated by Lt Col E. Woodhouse for the Ministry of Transport. His report, dated 17 December 1937, described the approach to the foot of the incline as a curve to the right of about 20 chains (¼ mile) radius, descending at 1 in 1056 for 160 yards. The incline was straight, rising at 1 in 60 and steepening to 1 in 20 and 1 in 14 at the top. The track had been relaid in 1925 with

NLR 0-6-0T 27521 derailed into the road near the foot of Hopton incline on 6 October 1937, still lying there on 14 October awaiting dismantling and removal *(H. Towneley)*

'serviceable' LNWR material. The 30ft rails, originally 90lb/yd, had worn down to about 81lb. On the curve there were 13 sleepers per rail length, measuring 12 x 6in in section. Elsewhere there were normally 12 sleepers 11 x 5in per rail length. The ballast was ash, and there was a super elevation of 6in on the curve to provide for the practice of rushing the incline.

The first sign of derailment was on the right rail near the end of the curve, caused by the wagon which stayed on the embankment. Its position in the train could not be definitely established. About 22 yards beyond here was a deep flange mark on the left rail, and other damage, suggesting that the engine and wagons rolled down the embankment. To the rear of the derailment the track had been displaced laterally, both to the right and left.

The engine was described as built by the North London Railway in 1892. It had run 17,427 miles since its wheels and axleboxes were last overhauled in August 1935. The wheels were 4ft 4in diameter, the wheelbase 11ft 4in; the engine was 27ft 10in long and weighed 45½ tons in working order. The parts of the engine were thoroughly examined at Derby and nothing was discovered that might have caused the derailment. The same applied to the wagons and brake van which were examined where they lay.

Driver T. Walker, giving evidence, stated that he had been driving on the High Peak line for 21 years and that it was his practice to go 'all out' for Hopton tunnel and to work up to a speed of 40 or even 50mph, and even then he had occasionally failed to reach the top of the incline at the first attempt. Trains had had to be divided, taken up in two parts, and reassembled in the siding at the top. He said that the NLR tanks tended to surge from side to side at speed.

Fireman Kirk, who had been injured in the accident, explained that he had worked on the line for 25 years and had been firing for Driver Boden, who was killed, for seven years. He said that Driver Boden's practice was similar to Driver Walker's. He reckoned the speed on the curve was usually about 45mph and about 50mph on leaving it. Driver Boden had reported as many as ten or twelve times in a year that the curve had been distorted. Three men who were in the brake van agreed that the speed had not been excessive, but one remarked that the engine was 'rocking rather badly' when approaching the curve.

Drivers generally preferred the 2-4-0 'Chopper' tanks and agreed that before the NLR tanks arrived, in 1930, there had never been any trouble on the curve, but the 2-4-0Ts were less powerful. Lt Col Woodhouse concluded that the NLR tanks with their outside cylinders, small wheels and short wheelbase were unsuitable for running at high speed and that rushing the incline in the manner described 'introduced an undesirable element of risk'. He recommended lowering the speed to a maximum of 30mph and reducing the load. He also recommended more careful maintenance of the track, particularly in wet weather when there was more danger of displacement.

Even the remote CHPR was not free from vandalism. On 3 March 1950 2-4-0T 58092 ran into the disused siding at Black Rocks on the Sheep Pasture top section and ploughed into the bank at the end after the points had been mischievously changed. The crew leapt clear and no-one was injured.

On 29 July 1955 0-4-0ST 47000 derailed and fell into a garden at Steeple Grange above Wirksworth, landing on its right side. Recovery was difficult. It involved a good deal of excavation and construction of a ramp of old sleepers and rails. The engine was rerailed on 1 August.

There are records of several persons being run down by trains or by wagons on inclines, though it was reported that there were no accidents in 1858 and from 1 July to 31 December 1859[4]. But the CHPR was not a safe railway to work on and the following examples make it clear that the utmost vigilance was needed at all times. On 1 November 1860 a fireman was run over and killed while he was uncoupling wagons. On 28 February 1861 a trespasser was run over and killed. On 20 February 1862 a 'plane man' was killed while 'incautiously greasing the line rope drawing a van up an incline'. We are not told where these accidents took place, but they could have been anywhere on the line. More recently a telegraph linesman, Raymond Roseblade, was killed by a wagon on Middleton incline[5].

The most frequent casualties, however, were sheep and lambs, many of which would leap over the walls, and there are constant references in the minutes to compensation being paid to farmers. On 16 June 1842 John Leonard was ordered to pay £10 to a farmer towards the loss of his horse which fell down the cutting at Fernilee. Seventeen years later, in September 1869, Smith was authorized to pay £5 compensation to a farmer, also at Fernilee, for a foal killed by jumping over a wall and falling down a rock cutting, probably near the same place.

One of the most dangerous places was (and still is!) the level crossing on the public road at Minninglow. On 15 July 1879 a farmer's horse and cart were destroyed in a collision with a train. He claimed £36 compensation. On 7 March 1918 a herd of cows was being driven across during a snow storm when several strayed onto the railway and were run into by a train. One was killed and of three injured one had to be slaughtered. Another accident occurred there on 24 November 1921 when four horses strayed onto the line. Two were killed and two injured by a train. On 24 May 1922 the LNWR Works Committee ordered that fences and cattle guards should be provided, at an estimated cost of £66.

In winter, snow was a constant problem on the summit section. In October 1832 Leonard was asked to construct a machine for clearing snow from the rails. (see p17) In January 1842 90-100 men took three days to clear a heavy fall of snow from the summit level. Repeated falls practically closed the railway for a whole week. From 15 to 19 January 1843 from 100 to 300 men were employed at a cost of over £125 to clear the heaviest fall in living memory.

On 19 February 1845 John Leonard wrote to Andrew Brittlebank, solicitor[6]:

The enclosed refers to the spoil banks on the side of the Haven Lodge Cutting which I have always considered as belonging to us, but the Steward persists in giving the tenants permission to get clay and turn their cattle upon it although it is enclosed <u>to us</u> and <u>from them.</u> You also recollect perhaps that a few years ago we expended £20 in planting the greater portion of it with larch as a protection against snow and if it be ours the other (portion) ought to be planted as well. They have not interfered with the planted portion.'

Haven Lodge cutting was south of Newhaven tunnel.

Drifting snow filling the cutting at the north end of Buxton tunnel may have been the reason for an order on 15 March 1843 for centring to be provided for the tunnel 'for doing any repair which may be required.' On 1 June a sub-committee consisting of William Jessop (brother of Josias), Captain Goodwin and A. Brittlebank inspected the tunnel. There is clear evidence, inside and above, that the tunnel was extended by 25 yards at the north end. Although no reference to this has been found, it was probably done in spring 1843, certainly before Captain Moorsom's survey of 1854.

Kitson 0-4-0ST 47000 after derailment into a garden at Steeplehouse on 29 July 1955 *(E.R. Morten)*

A combination of melting snow and continuous heavy rain caused the collapse of an embankment near Ladmanlow on 7 March 1881. A culvert became blocked and water filled the valley until the embankment was carried away. Heavy snow on 7-8 December 1882 blocked the line between Hindlow and Harpur Hill. Another heavy snowfall was recorded in the week beginning 18 February 1888. Two trains were snowed up. The crew of one survived on milk from churns in transit to Manchester.

On 17 February 1919 a heavy and continuous snowstorm fell in the Peak District, drifting to a depth of 5-8ft. Near Longcliffe a goods train broke in two and seven wagons and a brake van were left fast in the snow. The snowplough was sent out from Buxton but became snowed up before reaching Parsley Hay. Another engine sent out to help was also stuck fast. A large gang of men managed to get the traffic moving on the Ashbourne line by 11.00 the next day and on the High Peak line by 16.30. Relief was short-lived for on 19-21 March another heavy snowfall blocked the line between Longcliffe and Friden. Two engines from Longcliffe managed to force their way through the drifts with the help of another strong team of men and traffic was moving again by 17.30.

In more recent years the wartime winter in early 1940 created exceptional problems. In the severe winter of 1947, in February and March long sections of the line were closed by snowdrifts of great depth. Large numbers of Italian prisoners of war were employed in clearing the snow. Perhaps the worst of all was the long winter of January to March 1963 when traffic was stopped by snow on many occasions and the line was kept open only with the greatest difficulty.

NOTES

1. PRO/RAIL 410/180 LNWR Traffic Committee minute 18553 18 October 1876.
2. PRO/RAIL 144/1309.
3. LNWR Act 26 July 1889 c 98.
4. Notes from a log book kept at Middleton top.
5. *Derbyshire Advertiser* 25 July 1952.
6. PRO/RAIL 144/5.

Italian prisoners of war clearing snow in Minninglow cutting, March 1947

Buxton ploughs working at Dowlow on the Buxton - Ashbourne line, 27 February 1955. The locomotives are a 4F 0-6-0, Stanier 2-8-0 and and LNWR 0-8-0. The old CHPR track crossed diagonally here from lower right to left centre. (See photo on page 64)

(E.R. Morten)

9. Operating Regulations

As might be expected on a railway so beset with operating hazards as the CHPR, strict rules were soon enforced, but not before there had been several mishaps. The earliest printed rules still extant appear to be those in the form of a glazed poster signed by Francis Barton on 3 March 1853, a copy of which is in the Public Record Office at Kew[1]. It sheds a revealing light on working conditions during the period when the traffic was still operated by private carriers.

Inclined planes were to be kept at work 12 hours each day except Sundays when work stopped, and on Good Fridays and Christmas Days when they were stopped 'during the time of Divine Service'. Ascending wagons were not taken up the Sheep Pasture or Whaley inclines after noon, and up the others after 15.00. Drivers (presumably of horse-drawn trains, which were limited to 36 tons gross) had to remain at the inclines with their wagons, which were to be handled in order of arrival. Wagons were to be arranged so that the 'preventor' (sic) could be applied to the heaviest wagon. As soon as trains had passed over the inclines drivers were to remove them immediately. No driver was to allow any passenger or other person not employed on the railway to ride on his wagons on the inclines.

On single-line sections wagons which had passed the half-way mark were to be allowed to proceed, and those beyond were to turn back to the next turnout at not less than 3mph. Wagons being passed were to stand on the main line and the passing train was to use the turnout.

Four bye laws printed on the poster gave details of fines for various offences concerning the use and operation of wagons. The fourth ordered: 'That any driver or other person causing any wagon, loaded or unloaded, to be drawn along the railway, otherwise than upon the rails, shall, for each offence, forfeit and pay any sum not exceeding 20 shillings.' This survived into the rule book of 1877. A list of extracts from the 1825 Act was appended.

The first proper rule book was printed in 1858, following re-incorporation of the company. It consisted of 44 pages and was signed by William Smith. Every servant of the company was required to sign in a special book to indicate that he had 'read, or heard read, and understood,' the rule book.

Rules for the operation of the inclines made it clear that the engineman was wholly responsible for 'hangers-on' and 'planemen', and for the satisfactory condition of all wagons passing over an incline. No ascending train was to be allowed to pass without a preventer being applied to each wagon; and no descending train was to be let down 'without the descending preventer in advance having been carefully applied'. It is not clear how the 'preventer' worked on descending trains. On the inclines with curves (Sheep Pasture and Bunsall) wagons were to carry 'the proper implement to keep the rope down to the pulleys in the curves.' This was known variously as a 'cat', 'dog', 'elephant' and 'donkey'. The speed limit on the inclines was 8mph.

No person was allowed to ride up or down the inclines, and all passengers were made to wait until a descending train was in motion before they walked down the incline. Ascending trains were not to be drawn up until all the passengers had arrived at the top. On Sheep Pasture this could result in a delay of half an hour. The limits were two loaded wagons up or down and two empties going up. Each wagon was to have a separate tail chain fastening. Wagons were never to be coupled with the two fly wagons either up or down. Midland and LNWR wagons were to be passed up or down one at a time, loaded or empty. Loaded and empty wagons were not to be passed up or down together.

The engineman was to walk up and down the incline and examine all tail chains and hemp rope ends, tackling chains, pulleys, etc, every morning before starting work, and he was to sign his name in the book kept by a planeman at both the bottom and top of the incline. This could be an arduous duty in bad weather.

In the section headed 'Locomotive Engines' the rules allowed only one engine at a time on the Bunsall foot – Shallcross top and Bunsall top – Ladmanlow sections. This last section included Buxton tunnel. Apart from this there were no special rules for working the single-line sections. Rule 52 stated: 'The Engine Driver, when following the Fly Goods Train with his Train, not to advance nearer than 100 yards of the former.' By the 1870s there was a rule whereby a driver, before entering a section, must see the staff for that section. The staff was carried to the other end by the last train of a group of following trains. This was not enough to prevent the fatal collision in December 1875, mentioned earlier.

Other rules concerned Flymen, Slowmen, Platelayers, Signals, Trespassing, Reports and Complaints. An interesting rule in the section headed 'Slowmen' is No 83 which reads: 'On that part of the line where the reverse shunt is placed he must see the Waggons in his charge are all properly reversed, and placed on the line in the right position for going down the planes, accordingly as the Waggons are going towards Cromford or Whaley.' This rule probably refers to the triangle (GR 094685) close to the south end of the present Hindlow tunnel, on one of the sections abandoned in 1892, and at the summit of the line. It suggests that some wagons, perhaps with end doors, may have been suitable for travelling on inclines facing one way only, with the door at the upper end. Such wagons starting at Cromford or Whaley Bridge would most probably be empty. Some vans had doors on one side only and had to be turned to suit certain platforms and goods sheds.

The 1858 rule book remained in force until it was replaced by one dated 16 June 1877, issued by the LNWR for the Cromford & High Peak Line. The new rule book, also signed by William Smith, contained 84 pages. The standard of literacy was evidently still low: rule 5 stated 'In case any man is unable to read, the inspector or foreman must read and explain the Rules to him.'

A supplement dated October 1877 divided the line into nine sections regulated by engine staffs, as listed opposite.

The staff was to be suspended on the weather board of the engine and the driver was responsible for seeing it was in the right place before starting. Over sections 4a and 6 'Fly Trains' were still allowed to pass in either direction provided that both driver and fireman saw the staff for the section before entering it. The staffs were as follows:

No.	Section	Form of Staff	Colour
1.	High Peak Junction to Cromford	Square	Black
2.	Summit of Sheep Pasture to foot of Middleton	Circular	Red
3.	Summit of Middleton to summit of Hopton	Square	Green
4.	Summit of Hopton to foot of Hurdlow	Triangular	Yellow
4a.	Foot of Hurdlow to top of Hurdlow	Square	Blue
5.	Top of Hurdlow to Harpur Hill	Circular	Yellow & Blue
6.	Harpur Hill to Grinn Branch Junction	Triangular	Blue
7.	Colliery Junction to Bunsall	Square	White
8.	Foot of Bunsall to summit of Shallcross	Circular	Black

Engines were not to exceed 12mph. The list of sections worked under one engine in steam regulations was extended, probably as a result of the 1875 collision at Turncliffe, and was as follows: Shallcross top – Bunsall foot; Harpur Hill – Hurdlow top; Hurdlow foot – Hopton top; Hopton foot –

Station cottage at Longcliffe, c 1890

Railway family at Longcliffe, c 1890

Middleton top; Middleton foot – Sheep Pasture top; Cromford – High Peak Junction.

When a train was approaching the junctions with the Buxton line at Whaley Bridge or the Midland at High Peak Junction it was to stop at the distant signal and the flyman was to walk forward to obtain permission to proceed from the junction signalman.

The curious old names died hard. One can imagine a new curate asking a CHPR employee about his work and being told: 'I am a slowman' or 'a planeman' or 'a hanger-on'.

Wagons were 'hung on' to the rope by a tackling chain which was hooked onto the coupling at the lower end of the wagon, or of the lower wagon when ascending. The chain passed over the lower axle and under the upper axle or axles. The other end was attached to two tapering chains which were wound round the rope in opposite directions. The small ends were joined by leather straps. To keep the haulage rope in the guide pulleys on the curves on Sheep Pasture and Bunsall inclines the chain was held down by the 'donkey', a steel link hooked over the upper drawhook and retained centrally by chains to the buffers. (See photographs below). This was not necessary on the other inclines which were straight. Descending wagons were attached separately with a gap between them to allow for slack being taken up. If they did come together it could be hard work detaching them at the incline foot. A spare set of tackling chains always had to be sent up with ascending wagons.

The timetable on 1 April 1891, shortly before the end of the CHPR as a through route, shows the pattern of operation which had evolved. The principal trains are shown below.

There were also short trip workings to various quarries and lime works, and Goyt colliery near Burbage. Some of these trips were worked by Buxton Lime Co locomotives. Goyt colliery closed in 1902, but the track remained from Ladmanlow to the junction near the old Macclesfield road until August 1958.

Special instructions concerned the curious signals at Grinn Branch and Colliery junctions near Ladmanlow. On the signal posts with two arms, the upper arm was for 'main line engines' and the lower arm was for Buxton Lime Co engines.

'Breaksmen' were not to carry gunpowder from the Fernilee Works in their vans when there was a fire in the van.

To avoid delay to urgent goods and 'foreign wagons' received after despatch of the 11.30 Cromford to Shallcross train, the planeman at Sheep Pasture foot was to enquire at 4.00pm daily what traffic was to be sent to Middleton top. He was to place a 'Target' on the last wagon. All concerned were to see that the wagons were worked up ready for the 6.20 train from Cromford next morning. The planeman at Middleton top was to return the target promptly to Cromford.

The workings included delivery of water in four-wheeled tanks converted from old LNWR tenders.

WEEKDAYS	1	3	5C
Down Trains			
High Peak Junction			1.40
Cromford (Bottom)	6.20	11.30	2.00
Sheep Pasture (Top)	6.29	11.39	2.15
Steeplehouse	6.45	11.55	2.20
Middle Peak Yard	6.50	12.5	2.30
Middleton (Top)	7.00	12.20	2.40
Hopton (Top)	7.30	12.50	3.00
Manystones Siding	X	X	...
Longcliffe	7.53	1.30	3.8
Bloore's Siding	X	X	...
Minninglow Sidings	X	X	...
Friden	8.19	2.10	3.28
Parsley Hay	8.39	2.30	3.38
Hurdlow (Bottom)*	8.47	2.50	3.45
Hurdlow (Top)* ar	9.2	3.5	3.50
Hurdlow (Top) dp	9.7	3.15	...
Brigg's Siding	X	X	...
Hindlow	9.15	3.30	4.00
Harpur Hill	9.30	3.43	4.10
Ladmanlow	9.47	4.35	4.20
Bunsall (Top)	10.00	4.45	4.30
Shallcross (Bottom)	10.45	5.30	5.00
Whaley Bridge	11.5	...	5.10

C Conditional Train. Runs when required only.
X Stops when required for traffic purposes
* 1869 deviation.

WEEKDAYS	10	12	13C
Up Trains			
Whaley Bridge	6.30	...	10.10
Shallcross (Bottom)	7.00	11.40	10.20
Bunsall (Top)	7.50	1.40	11.00
Ladmanlow	8.5	2.00	11.10
Harpur Hill	X	X	11.20
Hindlow	8.30	2.30	11.30
Briggs' Siding	X	X	...
Hurdlow (Top)* ar	8.40	2.40	...
dp	9.20	3.15	11.38
Hurdlow (Bottom)*	9.30	3.25	11.50
Parsley Hay	9.50	3.40	11.58
Friden	10.2	3.50	12.7
Minninglow Sidings	X	X	...
Bloore's Siding	X	X	...
Longcliffe	11.0	4.30	12.33
Manystones Siding	X	X	...
Hopton (Top)	11.40	4.50	12.35
Middleton (Top)	12.00	5.00	12.45
Middle Peak Yard	12.10	5.10	12.55
Steeplehouse	12.20	5.15	1.00
Sheep Pasture (Top)	12.30	5.20	1.10
Cromford	12.40	5.30	1.25
High Peak Junction	...	...	1.35

Breaksman of No. 1 changes with Breaksman of No. 10 at Hurdlow (Top).

Breaksman of No. 3 changes with Breaksman of No. 12 at Hurdlow (Top).

'Hanger-on' inspecting tackling chain at foot of Sheep Pasture incline

Kitson 0-4-0ST 47000 going down Middleton incline after recovery from derailment, July 1955. Water tank coming up. *(E.R. Morten)*

Water tanks at Longcliffe, 30 April 1967 *(T.A. Fletcher)*

These were filled from a large tank supplied by a spring opposite the workshop at Cromford and were delivered at various points along the railway to supply stationary engines, locomotives and cottages. The tanks were balanced on the inclines by descending loads of stone and lime.

There were 21 old tenders in use, from McConnell, Ramsbottom and Webb locomotives, either four-wheelers or six-wheelers with the middle wheels removed. Six-wheeled vehicles were not allowed over the inclines, although locomotives were passed up and down. At the end many of the tenders were well over 100 years old. They carried water to:

Sheep Pasture Top	Stationary engine
Sheep Pasture Top	Locomotive shed
Middleton Top	Stationary engine
Middleton Top	Locomotive shed
Intake quarry	By contract
Longcliffe	Locomotive supply
Parsley Hay, Hartington	Cottages
Alsop en le Dale, Hurdlow	Cottages

After reconstruction from Dowlow to Parsley Hay the CHPR was re-measured from zero at Buxton to High Peak Junction, 24 miles 39yd. Hindlow Junction was 3 miles 917yd and from there to the junction with the old line at Harpur Hill was 1 mile 1111yd. Following closure from Ladmanlow to Shallcross in 1892 the remaining section was re-measured from zero at the buffers near the old Macclesfield road bridge north of Ladmanlow. In 1927 Hillhead quarry was opened above Hindlow and a siding connection was laid in from Harpur Hill along the abandoned CHPR formation. It was passed fit for traffic on 3 June 1927. The total length of the section from beyond Ladmanlow to Hillhead quarry was 3 miles 564yd.

In 1920 a halt was opened at Dowlow to serve the quarry. Although a private halt, it appeared in the public timetable from 4 November 1929. It was closed on 1 November 1954, but was still owned by the Downlow Lime & Stone Co Ltd.

NOTE

1. PRO RAIL 1001/34

'Hanger -on' detaching a wagon from the rope at the foot of Sheep Pasture incline, showing the 'donkey' which kept the rope down on the pulleys

Signal at Grin Quarry Siding, Ladmanlow

10. Into the second century

LNWR 2-4-0T 58092 passing Black Rocks, 5 June 1950. *(W.A. Camwell)*

On 1 January 1923 the LNWR became part of the London, Midland & Scottish Railway, but this had little effect on the traffic pattern on the CHPR. A set of special instructions for working the Sheep Pasture and Middleton inclines, issued by the LMS on 1 March 1937, was remarkably similar to those in the rule book of 1858. Maximum loads were: when balancing, 1 loaded or 3 empties up; 2 loaded or 5 empties down. When winding (that is, unbalanced load up or down) 2 loaded or 5 empties down. When winding (that is, unbalanced loads up or down) 2 loaded or 5 empties up or down. The maximum speed was still 8mph. The 'donkey' to hold the rope down to the pulleys on the curves had to be used on Sheep Pasture. Instructions to incline staff read as follows:

Planemen – *As soon as wagons are attached and are ready for a run, the planeman at the bottom of the incline must set the signal to the 'go' position. As soon as the run has started up the incline the signal must be set back to 'stand' position.*

Hangers-on – *As soon as wagons are attached and are ready for a run, the hanger-on at the top of the incline must satisfy himself that the planeman at the bottom is ready before taking off his semaphore signal and knocking out the turn-on scotches. As soon as the run has started, the semaphore signal must be put back to the 'danger' position.*

The hanger-on is responsible for attaching chains to wire rope; after knocking off the turn-on scotches he must not take off the semaphore signal until he has satisfied himself that each chain (where the weight descending exceeds 19 tons) bears its proportionate weight.

Engineman – *The engineman must on no account allow a run to start without first seeing that the indicator in the engine room and semaphore at the top of the incline, are both set to the 'go' position. He must see that the indicator and semaphore are set back after the run has started. The 'drum' brake in the engine house must be put on immediately on completion of a run and must not be removed till the semaphore is taken off and indicator set to 'go'.*

Middleton Fireman – *The fireman is responsible for taking off chains from the ascending wagons on completion of a run, and laying these ready for the hanger-on to put on descending wagons. When a signal for the run is given from the bottom, he must come out and stand near the top of the incline, ready to give a signal to the engineman if anything goes wrong.*

If it is necessary to lower or pull up wagons on the incline without wagons being attached to the rope on the other road, a load not exceeding 20 tons may be allowed to ascend at a time.

The brake must be pinned down on the descending load, and special precautions taken to regulate the speed of the winding engine accordingly.

The gross weight of a run is taken at 38 tons, and this load must not be exceeded.

It may be necessary from time to time through weather etc to reduce the above loads, and in that case the responsibility for seeing this is done will be in the hands of the Locomotive Representative.

No wagons are to be moved at the top of the incline by means of the winding rope except those directly attached to it.

Further special instructions governed the working of the points to the catch pit on Sheep Pasture incline:

The planeman in charge at the foot of Sheep Pasture incline will be held responsible for seeing that the man appointed to work the points leading to the catch pit is at his post, and that the points are in good working order, before allowing any wagons to be moved either up or down the incline. When commencing duty each day the planeman must go to the cabin *to see that the man appointed to work the points is at his post, and the planeman must also test the working of the points to satisfy himself that they are in good order.*

The points in their normal position stand open, leading to the catch pit, and will require to be held firmly over, to allow the wagons to pass to the bottom of the incline.

The pointsman must carefully observe the descending wagons as they approach and when satisfied from the speed at which the wagons are travelling that they are attached to the rope, he must hold the points firmly and securely over.

After sunset, or at any time when the wagons cannot be seen for a distance of at least 100yd, the planeman in charge at the top of the incline will be held responsible for securely fixing a lamp on the front of the leading wagon descending the incline. The lamp must be so placed as to show a red light to the front.

A gong, worked by two treadles, is placed near the pointsman's cabin. One of the treadles is fixed 100yd from the cabin, and the other 200yd from the cabin. As the wagons pass over the treadles the gong will sound, and the pointsman must carefully observe the interval between the strokes on the gong, and by this means he will be able at any time (when he cannot see the wagons or the lamp fixed upon them) to ascertain if they are attached to the rope and travelling at the ordinary speed.

Electric bell communication is provided between the pointsman's cabin and the engine house at the top of the incline (it was installed in 1890), and in case the rope should slip off the rollers, or it should become necessary from any cause for the engine to be stopped, the pointsman must immediately make use of the electric bell, and continue to do so until the engine has been stopped.

As soon as the bell in the engine house rings, the man in charge must stop the engine at once, and it must not again be set in motion until he has ascertained that all is in order.

The electric bell must be tested each morning, before the engine commences to work, by the pointsman giving six strokes on the bell, and the engineman will reply by giving the same number of strokes.

The line was operated as follows:

High Peak Junction to Cromford Goods	OES
Sheep Pasture top to Middleton foot	OES
Middleton top to Hopton foot	TS&T
Hopton top to Longcliffe	TS&T
Longcliffe to Friden	TS&T
Friden to Parsley Hay	TS&T
Parsley Hay to Hurdlow Double Track	AB
Briggs' Siding to Hindlow Double Track	AB
Hindlow to Harpur Hill	TS&T
Harpur Hill to Old Harpur as goods yard	
Old Harpur to Ladmanlow	OES

OES	One engine in steam
TS&T	Train staff and ticket
AB	Absolute Block

Indicator in Middleton engine house. B = Stand By; G = Go; S = Stop

Indicator at Middleton foot, 13 June 1951

The first passenger train for many years was a six-coach excursion arranged by The Manchester Society of Engineers[1] which ran from Buxton to Friden on 18 June 1932, behind a Midland 3F 0-6-0. Friden was the limit of operation of locomotives from Middleton top. Here traffic was exchanged with locomotives from Buxton which also worked the Hindlow – Ladmanlow traffic. The CHPR remained busy throughout World War II and into nationalisation on 1 January 1948. Its future seemed so assured that various modernisation works were projected and even carried out.

A negative outcome of the modernisation was the closure of Whaley Bridge canal yard together with the whole line beyond the connection from Whaley Bridge station. This section was last used on 9 April 1952. The incline, nearly 121 years after its opening, was still worked by an endless chain. The rails remained until 1961. The bridge under the Buxton line was filled in in 1963. The Grinn Quarry branch was closed in the early 1950s.

Hurdlow station was closed on 15 August 1949. Parsley Hay to Dowlow was converted to single line on 2 June 1959. The last ramblers' excursion from Manchester called at Parsley Hay on 5 August 1962. Parsley Hay station was demolished in 1966.

By now enthusiasts' excursions over branch lines had become popular. The Stephenson Locomotive Society, North Western Area, and the Manchester Locomotive Society, arranged the first enthusiasts' special over the CHPR which ran on 25 April 1953. The tour started from Cromford Canal wharf from where the 'passengers' walked up Sheep Pasture incline. At the top 0-4-0ST 47000 took them to Middleton foot in open wagons. They then walked down to Wirksworth, travelled by train to Duffield and back, walked up to Middleton top and from there travelled in open wagons to Hopton top behind NLR 0-6-0 tanks 58860 and 58856. (See photograph). The last took the train to Friden. Here they joined a train of coaches behind MR 3F 0-6-0 43618 which ran right through to Ladmanlow and back to Hindlow from where it returned with the train to Buxton. The tour was so popular that it had to be repeated on 27 June. Altogether the SLS, sometimes in conjunction with the MLS, ran six tours over the CHPR, the last on Sunday 30 April 1967, a week after the official end of traffic. Excursions were also run by other societies.

Old Harpur to Ladmanlow closed on 2 August

Driver Sam Buckley on a J94 0-6-0ST. He spent his entire working life on the CHPR.

1954 and demolition began in August 1958. The bridge over the A54 Buxton – Macclesfield road was demolished at about the same time. The last track was cut up in March 1967.

Until Middleton engine shed was closed one engine worked Hopton top to Friden, the other Intake and Hopton Wood quarries and up to Hopton top. After closure they were transferred to Buxton. In May 1964 Cromford shed became a sub shed of Derby.

The last new rope was installed on Middleton incline on 4 September 1957. Plans were prepared for replacing the Middleton stationary engine but, fortunately, before this could be carried out, the Hopton Wood quarry closed on 16 June 1962 and the Middleton incline was last used on 31 May 1963. The engine was restored by the Middleton Engine Group and the Industrial Archaeology Section of the Derbyshire Archaeological Society with assistance from the County Council. It is classed as an ancient monument.

Traffic on the Sheep Pasture top section and going down Sheep Pasture incline, however, amounted to 60,785 tons in 1961 and produced net receipts of £16,534[2]. It was stated that quarries in the same area had limestone deposits sufficient for the next 100 years and it was expected that the rail traffic would be increased to 100,000 tons a year which justified retention of Sheep Pasture incline. The old DX 0-6-0 engine and winding equipment could have been repaired at a cost of £6,500, but it was estimated that all the 13-ton wagons would be withdrawn by 1970 and that the ability to handle only one 16-ton wagon at a time would necessitate double shift working and artificial lighting for working after dark

It was therefore proposed to replace the winding machinery by electrical gear with a capacity of 100 tons, or four loaded 16-ton wagons. So the old steam engine and boiler were replaced by an electric motor installed at a cost of £31,700 by John Boyd & Co (Engineers) Ltd of Annan, and brought into use in September 1964.

While this work was in progress traffic from Middleton quarry was worked by road down to Wirksworth where it was loaded into 25 ton hopper wagons. These could not be used on Sheep Pasture incline because of the narrow width between the tracks. The new operation proved so much more economical that it was eventually decided to work it all via Wirksworth and out by the former Midland branch to Duffield. The last wagons were worked down Sheep Pasture incline on 1 April 1967. The remaining sections of the CHPR were closed later that year. The new electrical winding machinery was discarded, and now the Wirksworth branch has been abandoned the stone traffic is carried by heavy lorries along the twisting narrow roads. The water tanks on the high-level siding at Longcliffe were removed on 2 May 1967. The table below shows the various closure dates.

NLR 0-6-0T 58860 shunting at Friden, 5 June 1950

2. 1.1869 Hurdlow foot to Dowlow via incline
27. 6.1892 South of Hindlow tunnel to Harpur Hill; Old Macclesfield road, Ladmanlow, to Shallcross foot
15. 8.1949 Hurdlow station
2. 4.1951 Higher Buxton station
10. 4.1952 Whaley Bridge Peak Forest Canal to junction with 1857 connection
2. 8.1954 Ladmanlow station and to 380 yards east of Ministry of Fuel & Power sidings
1.11.1954 Buxton – Ashbourne (passengers)
21. 6.1959 Parsley Hay to Briggs' Siding singled
12. 6.1962 Hopton Wood Quarry branch
3. 6.1963 Middleton top to Steeplehouse (Middleton incline)
7.10.1963 Ashbourne to Hartington (final closure)
6. 7.1964 Friden closed to parcels and freight, reduced to coal depot
2.12.1964 Middle Peak Wharf (Middleton foot) to Middleton Quarry branch junction
1. 2.1965 Whaley Bridge station to Shallcross yard
9. 2.1966 Harpur Hill to Old Harpur, final siding closed
2. 1.1967 Parsley Hay to Hartington (goods)
5. 9.1967 Parsley Hay to Hartington (water traffic)
3. 4.1967 High Peak Junction to Steeplehouse and Middleton Stone Quarry
1. 5.1967 Middleton top to Friden
17. 9.1967 High Peak Junction signal box
2.10.1967 Dowlow Siding, Hindlow, to Parsley Hay and Hartington
21.11.1967 Parsley Hay to Friden put out of use
19. 9.1973 Hillhead Quarry to Harpur Hill and Hindlow Junction

The first abandoned section to be acquired by another body was from the bridge under the present A5002 Whaley Bridge to Buxton road at Fernilee to the north end of Buxton tunnel, which was bought by Stockport Corporation on 12 June 1936 in connection with the Fernilee reservoir in the Goyt valley. Later Stockport & District Water Board acquired an interest in the portion of the Buxton tunnel from beneath the watershed to the north end, about two thirds of the length.

Following closure and dismantling of the CHPR and the Parsley Hay – Ashbourne line the Peak Park Planning Board purchased the 11½ miles from Ashbourne to Hartington in 1968 and began developing it as the 'Tissington Trail'. This was opened to the public on 5 June 1971. The remaining sections within the National Park: Hartington to Parsley Hay, 1½ miles, and the CHPR from the NP boundary at Daisy Bank near Longcliffe to just north of the boundary near Dowlow, 10½ miles, were purchased in April 1971 and opened to the public in May 1972. The southern section, from the NP boundary to High Peak Junction, about 7 miles, was acquired by Derbyshire County Council for development as a trail and was officially opened on 16 March 1974, though the public had been walking along it since 1967.

Two NLR 0-6-0 tanks on SLS/MLS rail tour climbing Hopton incline 25 April 1953 *(E.R. Morten)*

The last abandoned section of the CHPR to change ownership was the southern third of Buxton tunnel and from there to the old Macclesfield road, acquired by Post Office Telecommunications in 1974 for an underground cable. It acquired easements from the Earl of Derby and the Water Authority to carry the cable through the tunnel and along the track to the foot of Bunsall incline. From Shallcross foot to Whaley Bridge the trackbed has been preserved and developed by the local district council.

NOTES

1. Not Mather & Platt, as confirmed by letter from G.O. Holt, 11 July 1982
2. Memorandum to London Midland Railway Board, 28 January 1963

SLS/MLS rail tour at Middleton foot, 4 March 1967 *(John Marshall)*

SLS/MLS rail tour train at Harpur Hill, 22 April 1961. 2-6-4T 42371
(John Marshall)

J94s 68006 and 68012 at Newhaven level crossing heading towards Middleton top with SLS brake van special, 30 April 1967. The crossing keeper's house on the right was later demolished. *(T.A. Fletcher)*

Operating over part of the 1 in 27 Killers branch from Steeplehouse towards Middleton Village, the Steeple Grange Light Railway is a 1'6" gauge line using former mining and quarrying equipment. The picture shows Greenwood & Batley battery loco No. 6061 of 1961 standing at Dark Lane quarry platform on 6 July 1996.
(Martin Bairstow)

11. Along the course of the railway

The Cromford & High Peak today. John Holroyd has hired a bike at Parsley Hay and is now less than a mile into the 14 mile trip to Middleton Top. *(P. Lockwood)*

After the total closure of the CHPR the first 17½ miles from High Peak Junction was made into the High Peak Trail for walkers and cyclists. Much of the remaining 15½ miles is walkable to Whaley Bridge, but long diversions are necessary in places round quarries and farmland.

From High Peak Junction the track runs on a ledge above the right bank of the Derwent with a good view of the Wigwell aqueduct on the right. It comes alongside the Cromford Canal opposite the Leawood Pump House. The wharf warehouse between the railway and the canal is now an educational centre with residential accommodation. The base of the old hand crane is still in place.

At the end of the section beside the canal, in what is now the picnic site, there was an engine shed for the locomotive used between here and the junction. The line turned sharp left at the level crossing by the canal swing bridge and passed in front of the workshop. This building, open to the public, contains the only remaining cast iron rails still in their original position, along the inspection pit. An old signal post stands beside the end of the workshop. Opposite this was the large water tank used to fill the old tenders in which the water was transported to various sites along the railway. The former CHPR agent's house stands beside the A6 road above.

At the foot of the Sheep Pasture incline, in front of the workshop building, is the pit containing the 9ft 6in diameter tensioning pulley. The old indicator with the letters 'B', 'G', 'S' (Stand By, Go, Stop) has been restored. Immediately above here the A6 road was carried over the two tracks by a skew elliptical arch. The present arched 'tunnel' was built in 1981, 14 years after removal of the track, to enable the road to be widened. The tracks diverged just above here and passed each side of the catch pit, installed in 1889 (see p68). Inside is the wreckage of a wagon which ran away in September 1965. To the right above here the embankment is supported by a massive stone retaining wall.

Half way up the incline, where it curves to the right, there is a cleared space on the right and a small shed. Opposite this, to the left of the incline, is a hollow containing a few dressed stones, all that remains of the intermediate engine house abandoned in 1857. Originally the gradient eased here to provide a place to transfer the wagons from one endless chain to the other. At the incline top the stationary engine house still stands, an empty shell. The flue from the boilers can be found by

Foot of Sheep Pasture incline. Cromford workshops on left. Water tanks about to ascend.
(D.W.K. Jones)

Engine shed, stationary engine reservoir and engineman's house at Middleton top; NLR 0-6-0T 58860 outside shed, 5 June 1950
(W.A. Camwell)

scrambling up the rocks above, or by going up the steps and turning left at the top. The reservoir for the engine water is on the left. There was also a wooden engine shed and cylindrical water tank for the locomotives.

The view to the right from here is the finest of any from the railway. Cromford is laid out immediately below with Riber Castle above across the Derwent Valley. In the distance High Tor towers above Matlock. Soon we come to Black Rocks, on the left. An enjoyable scramble to the top is rewarded by splendid views. Black Rocks Siding was on the left. Cromford Moor Siding, also on the left, was about 180 yards further on.

The track turns right onto a stone-faced embankment, crossing over two roads by arch bridges, and leading to the junction of the Killers branch. This half-mile branch turned off right and up a gradient of 1 in 27 for 1110 yards to Middleton quarry. Steeplehouse goods yard was on the left of the junction. The line turned left, then right. Coales Hill quarry on the right was served by a siding. Over the wall on the left (GR284552) is the top of the former Midland incline from Wirksworth. Most of it has now been quarried away. Just beyond, the Middle Peak quarry branch turned off to the left. Middle Peak Wharf, also situated here, was closed on 2 March 1964.

We now arrive at Middleton incline foot where there is the pit containing the tensioning pulley. A short distance up a stone arch carried the incline over the B5023 road. The bridge over the rock cutting beyond here carried an exciting road between two quarry faces, but all this has now been quarried away. Above the bridge, on the left, is the quarry worked from 1857 by William Wheatcroft and served by one, or two, sidings (see p00), resulting in the singling of the track from 1857 to 1894. There has been so much disturbance of the ground that it is difficult to work out how the siding arrangement might have been. The incline crosses a lane by a cast-iron span whose girders replaced the originals in 1865-66 (see p51). Part of the incline embankment was cut through above here in 1980 for a new road to by-pass the old bridge, and a new bridge was built for the track.

The most important feature at Middleton top is the engine house and stationary engine. The engine, restored by the Derbyshire Industrial Archaeology Society is administered by Derbyshire County Council and is under the care of the Warden. The engine house is open to the public on Sundays, and the engine is 'steamed' (on compressed air) on the first Saturday in each month. Samples of the 4ft and 3ft cast-iron rails may be seen, together with stone block sleepers, pulleys and other equipment. The 6ft diameter pulleys round which the rope passed into and out of the engine house are still in place.

As explained on p28, in 1857 the engine was rebuilt with a drum for a single tail rope when the incline was converted to single track. New cylinders and valve gear were installed in 1870. In March 1894 the engine was rebuilt to its original form and a new drum wheel was fitted. In April 1900 it had a new left-hand piston and in May 1901 a new right-hand one. A new 14ft friction wheel was installed on 21 April 1905; a broken drive shaft was replaced on 1 October 1905; a new 4ft pulley and a new 'winding out gear pinion' were fitted in December 1906; and a new cylinder bottom joint was made on 28 April 1907. In 1908 new RH piston rings were put in on 3 May; new air pump pistons were fitted on 2 June and on 26 September a new clutch pinion was fitted. Following an accident a new air pump crosshead was installed on 26 March 1909 and on 18 April new brake blocks and 4ft pulley were fitted. On 16 May the RH piston was 'put to work after repairs' and on 25 March 1910 a new RH cylinder and piston were installed. New 30ft long timbers were fixed under the straining wheel at the bottom on 25 September 1910. A new LH cylinder and piston were fitted on 14 April 1911 and on 11 June a new crank shaft.

Later, on 26 November, a new regulator was fitted. A new pinion was fitted on 1 September 1912 and a new worm wheel and pinion on 25 December. There is no record of further renewals and changes until a new 14ft upper friction wheel was installed by BR engineers from Derby in 1962. After all this metamorphosis there cannot be a great deal of the original engine left. It can be stated with reasonable certainty that the beams, connecting rods and parallel motions are as originally installed. Beneath the engine house is a well 192ft down to the water surface.

On the left, looking down the incline, a notice displayed the following 'poem in free verse':

Staff must exercise great care
When walking up or down the incline
And keep a sharp lookout
For movement of the wire rope.
When the rope starts to move
Staff must stop and stand clear
Of approaching wagons.
No one must remain within
The 'Danger Zone' notice boards
In the centre of the incline
When wagons are moving.

The engineman's house has been modernised for the warden's accommodation, and the original Butterley Co cast-iron window frames were replaced. (Will the replacements last 140 years?). The engine house still has the Butterley Co cast-iron doors and window frames. The reservoir has been drained and made into a picnic area. The site also provides car parking and toilet facilities; the warden has an office and shop where leaflets etc can be obtained. Cycles may be hired here. Opposite the car park is Redhill quarry, once served by a siding.

Just beyond Middleton top is another embankment with stone sides, pierced by a cattle arch. Intake quarry on the right was served by a siding. Soon we reach Hopton tunnel, 113yd long, 20ft wide, partly unlined, with deep rock cuttings at each end. Beyond here, on the right, the former

Via Gellia bridge near Hopton foot, GR 262546, 15 May 1980 *(John Marshall)*

Inscribed stone on south face of Via Gellia bridge, 5 May 1980. The inscription reads: 'Emma Matilda Wilmot laid this stone May XX MDCCCXXVII' *(John Marshall)*

Embankment at GR 205574 near Nine Miles Plantation, from SLS/MLS tour train, 22 April 1961 *(John Marshall)*

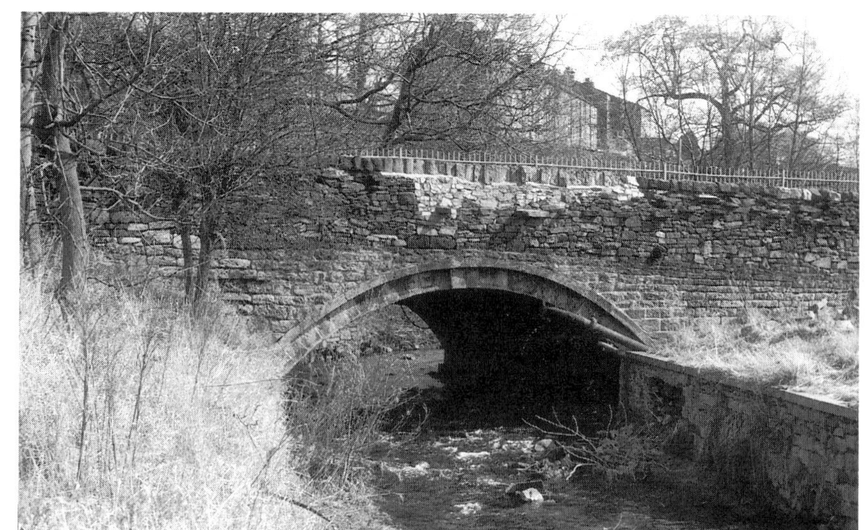

CHPR bridge over Randall Carr Brook near Shallcross, 3 April 1980 *(John Marshall)*

Bunsall incline, abandoned 1892. The middle stationary engine, in use until 1857, was on the left by the level embankment where wagons were transferred between upper and lower chains and where there are still many stone sleeper blocks in place. The former engine-man's house, on the right, was demolished about 1950. *(LGRP)*

Bridge near foot of Bunsall incline, GR 018758, 10 March 1956 *(Harold D. Bowtell)*

Hopton Wood quarry branch trailed in. Opposite the junction, on the left, is the remains of a wagon-type boiler (straight sides, semi-circular top, flat bottom) and what may be the base of an engine installed in 1857 to work wagons up the incline from the quarry (see p28). It is not known when rope haulage was last used and the working taken over by LNWR locomotives. Hopton incline can be seen ahead. The track crosses the head of the Via Gellia valley, GR263546, by a stone arch into which three inscribed stones have been built. At ground level on the north-east abutment is a stone laid by Lady Scarsdale on 14 November 1826. About 10ft up on the south-west abutment is a stone laid by Emma Matilda Wilmot on 20 May 1827, and on the north-west abutment another laid by Emma Thornhill on 18 May 1827. Lord Scarsdale, who lived at Mackworth Castle, near Derby, owned the house *Oddo* occupied by William Brittlebank, solicitor to the CHPR. William Pole Thornhill was a magistrate at Stanton near Youlgreave. The Wilmot connection has not been discovered. At the foot of Hopton incline was the 'Bone Works Siding' on the right. In 1963 a new factory was opened here by Magnesium Electron Ltd, but it was not a success and it was closed on 20 June 1966. A new works now occupies the site. No trace remains of the stationary engine house at the top of the incline, but the site of the reservoir can be seen. Cyclists should ride up Hopton incline to appreciate the work done by the steam locomotives.

A siding on the right, GR251546, served Hopton Mining Co, and half a mile further, at GR242552, Harborough Siding served Swann Ratcliffe's firebrick works. At GR238555 Manystones Siding trailed in from the left. It was removed on 19 February 1941. Remains of the lime kilns can still be seen. A big rock cutting at GR235556 was frequently blocked by snowdrifts and can be flooded. Beyond Peak Quarry (left) the arch bridge over the road at GR228555 was demolished in May 1980. A sharp curve to the right leads past Longcliffe quarry and past a ramp, GR226556, on which two water tenders used to supply locomotives. At Longcliffe, GR226557, the goods shed still stands. On 30 June 1835 the warehouse here was consigned to Wheatcroft & Sons. The dwelling house remained in possession of Samuel Frost, Wirksworth[1]. A siding (right) to a quarry was removed on 30 June 1942. The station master's house is still occupied.

The track crosses the Ashbourne road by another cast-iron bridge similar to that on the Middleton incline, also erected in 1865 to replace the original cast-iron girders. Another quarry (right) was served by a siding, removed on 14 October 1950.

The $5\frac{1}{4}$ miles from Longcliffe to Friden were notable for sharp curves, three of 3 chains and one, at Gotham, $2\frac{1}{2}$ chains radius. On the long straight beyond Longcliffe, at GR223559, is a high stone-faced embankment. At GR220561 is another rock cutting.

Another stone-faced embankment with buttresses and an arch under follows at GR218563. At the National Park boundary, GR214562, is a curious underbridge consisting of two tall arches through a stone-faced embankment. The eastern arch is maintained by Derbyshire County Council and the western one by the Peak District National Park. The high stone arch at GR206568 has parapets formed of old stone block sleepers. Just beyond, on the left, a long siding branched off to serve a quarry worked by the Sheepbridge Coal & Iron Co. Beyond, at GR205574, are some old lime kilns on the right.

At Minninglow, GR205575, is another high stone-faced embankment. Just beyond it, on the right, the remains of a crane stand on a siding which served a quarry, GR205576. A rock cutting is followed by another stone-faced embankment, pierced by an arch, at GR196582. The blind level crossing at Minninglow, GR195581, was the scene of the collision with a horse and cart in 1879 and with a herd of cows in 1918 and some horses in 1921 (see p71). A minor road passes under an arch bridge at GR194582.

A rock cutting brings us to an embankment, stone-faced on the north side, with extensive views of woods and valleys. The famous Gotham curve, GR187584, with a radius of 140ft was the sharpest on the CHPR and it limited the types of locomotives and rolling stock. It had a superelevation of $10\frac{1}{8}$in, in 1945 reduced to $\frac{5}{8}$in. Three more sharp curves follow, and more fine views. At GR182597 we cross the Newhaven – Cromford road, A5012, and at GR172608 a stone arch carries the line over the B5056 road and into Friden. Here the Derbyshire Silica Firebrick Co built its works on the site of the old railway yard. Milk was loaded at a platform, and a 15in gauge railway ran to a quarry. The cutting at GR154628 is crossed by one of the few stone overbridges on the CHPR.

The next feature of interest is Newhaven tunnel, 51yd long. Above the south face is a stone plaque showing a wagon in the centre surrounded by the words 'Cromford & High Peak Railway 1825', and in the corners the letters 'P H & Co', thought to be the initials of the contractor, but the only contractor known on this length was Porteus & Co. Could it be Philip Heacock who was in the committee formed at the meeting on 16 June 1824 and who, in 1829, was agent to the Duke of Devonshire? We may never know. The date, 1825, was that of the first Act, well before construction began. On the north face another plaque also shows a wagon and beneath it the Latin motto 'Divina Palladis Arte' (By the divine skill of Pallas or Minerva, the Greek goddess of engineering). Around it is a circular inscription: 'Cromford & High Peak Railway Comp^{y}' 'Incorporated 1825'. Beneath is the name 'Wm Brittlebank Esqr' (the company's solicitor). a rectangular stone at the top, which appears to be of later date, is inscribed 'Jos^{s} Jessop Esqr, Engineer'. The plaques are not dated and there is no record of their installation. Jessop died in 1826, over $3\frac{1}{2}$ years before the railway was completed; the stone

Train on Minninglow embankment, at GR 197583, NLR 0-6-OT 58860, 5 June 1950 *(W.A. Camwell)*

Rounding Gotham curve behind J94 68013 on SLS/MLS rail tour, 22 April 1961 *(John Marshall)*

Weigh bridge at Parsley Hay, looking towards Buxton, 1 September 1968 *(T.A. Fletcher)*

was probably installed as a memorial.

Beyond the cutting the junction with the Tissington trail comes into view and in another quarter mile we are at Parsley Hay. Here there are toilet and cycle hiring facilities, car park and picnic site, and convenient access to the A515 Buxton – Ashbourne road.

On the Parsley Hay – Dowlow stretch there is much evidence of the re-alignment of 1894. The original line passed round the east side of the goods yard at Parsley Hay and there is another deviation between GR136644 and 131647 where two sharp curves were eliminated. There is another at GR130654 and between here and Hurdlow station.

From Hurdlow station, GR127661, the High Peak Trail follows the deviation route of 1869 to the end of the trail at the 'green lane' at GR111674, just beyond the National Park boundary. The original line abandoned in January 1869 turned sharp left at the station and climbed the Hurdlow incline. This can be followed on foot. At the top is a deep hollow, all that remains of the stationary engine house. Beyond the site of the level crossing at GR114667 a rock cutting has been filled in with 'night soil' from Bakewell, and a quarry beyond, which in the 1940s cut across the track, has been levelled. The track is joined again at GR114670 and can be followed to the junction of the 1869 line. Here the remains of a ramp can be seen on the left. This is the point at which the photograph was taken of the Crewe Goods 2-4-0 beneath the two water tenders (p56).

At Dowlow we come to the terminus of the railway from Buxton to Dowlow limeworks. The old CHPR track, abandoned in 1892, can be joined again at the bridge at the end of the lane from Sterndale Moor, GR097684, where another interesting deviation can be seen. Walkers can go along the south-west side of the railway to join the old track which can be followed to the site of the reversing triangle, GR095685.

The railway can be crossed by the bridge just south east of Hindlow tunnel and the original track rejoined for a muddy walk round Brierlow along the 1266ft contour. Above the north end of Hindlow tunnel the track disappears in a wilderness of quarry waste, dumped over the track since 1966. It is possible to walk the approximate course of the line past Hindlow quarry.

Six CHPR cottages still stand near the long-demolished bridge over the Longnor road at GR086689. The track can be rejoined here, but it soon disappears again in the waste tips of Buxton and Hillhead quarries for over a mile. A short stretch of embankment re-appears at GR076692 to cross a quarry track by an arch known as 'barrel bridge'. The track resumes at GR072697. There are ways round this section, using roads and tracks which the walker can find on the map. Permission should be obtained before venturing through the quarries where there is frequent blasting. The track of the 1892 line from Hindlow can be seen below on the right climbing at 1 in 41 to join the original route at Harpur Hill Junction, GR067706. The old track from here back to Hillhead quarry, abandoned in 1892, was reopened in 1927 (see p77).

The next section, from Harpur Hill to Ladmanlow is an interesting walk. Numerous sidings served industrial premises. At GR059707 there was a large underground mushroom farm. The site of Harpur Hill limeworks is now occupied by research laboratories of Sheffield University. Here we come to the site of the Harpur Hill deviation completed in 1875 (see p62). It began at GR059707 where the original line curved left to serve the Buxton Lime Co works. The deviation went straight ahead and at GR056705 crossed the original course which passed round the hill to the right. A connection was put in here to serve the limeworks. The deviation line passed through a rock cutting to cross the original track again at GR054704. Part of the old course beyond here was used by the Safety in Mines Research Station, dating from 1925. A new 1200ft explosion gallery was opened in 1965. The last train delivering coal to the research station ran on 24 January 1966. A track leads to the south end of this at GR054699 and from here the original line can be followed to the junction of the old and later tracks at GR049701. The 1875 line comes in along a high curving embankment. This was the site of the head-on collision in 1875 (see p68). Further realignment can be seen near Anthony Hill.

Stanley Moor reservoir appears on the right. Northwards from here to Ladmanlow track was removed in 1958; southwards to Harpur Hill in September 1966. Just before the site of the former level crossing over the A53 Buxton – Leek road, GR041717, the Grin quarry branch trailed in from the right. It was opened by the Buxton Lime Co in 1856 and closed in the early 1950s. Ladmanlow, once one of the principal stations on the CHPR, was closed in 1954. The level crossing was removed on 18 August 1958. Beyond here, the skew bridge over the A54 Buxton – Macclesfield road, renewed in 1865, was removed in 1958. It was a wrought-iron plate-girder through span. A little further on at Colliery Junction a branch curved off left to Goyt Colliery, closed in 1902. The stone arch carrying the old Macclesfield road over the track was filled in in 1974. From 1892 until August 1958 this was the 'end of track'. The zero milepost was by the buffer stop. (see photograph p64).

A pleasant walk leads to the south end of Buxton, or Burbage, tunnel. As mentioned earlier, this now accommodates an underground telecommunications cable, and it has a locked door at each end. There is no public right of way over the top. The tunnel is stone-lined throughout and is completely sound except that the north portal needs rebuilding where about 7ft of the extension gradually collapsed during the 1950s and '60s. This section was the highest on the line, cutting the 1300ft contour in several places at both sides of the tunnel. Walkers are advised to retrace their steps to the lane, now on their left. At the road junction turn

Bridges between Hurdlow and Parsley Hay, GR 139641. Near is 1830 bridge, beyond 1898, 24 April 1973 *(John Marshall)*

Ladmanlow yard, 6 July 1932 *(J.R. Hollick)*

Arch at GR 012806 carrying A625 road over CHPR between Shallcross and Whaley Bridge, looking towards Shallcross, 24 July 1962 *(John Marshall)*

left past Edgemoor to GR036738 where a path to the left leads over the moor to the north end of the tunnel.

From here the track bears right, round the head of a wild valley. At GR033747 a sharp curve was eliminated by a section of high embankment built about 1856. Several old stone sleeper blocks can still be found on the old 1831 embankment. At GR024752 the old railway embankment formed a dam for the Bunsall top reservoir. At the former level crossing the CHPR track becomes part of the road built in 1966 to provide access to the Errwood dam works. Until this time the foundations of the Bunsall top engine house could be explored, but the area has been levelled.

The view from the top of the incline is magnificent, with the Fernilee reservoir forming the most prominent feature. To the right of the curve half way down the incline, GR020757, there are plenty of remains of the intermediate stationary engine house and reservoir, abandoned in 1857. Here there are prominent remains of the level section where wagons were transferred from one chain to the other, with stone sleeper blocks still in place.

Just below here, on the left, is a stone monument incorporating a stone sleeper block and an inscribed plaque presented by the Stephenson Locomotive Society in 1972, and dedicated on 7 January 1973 to the commemoration of the former incline. The road bends left to the dam. Below the turn an overbridge has been filled in with the same disregard for railway relics as was shown at the top of the incline. A path leads down to the incline foot. Above, to the left, is Errwood dam, built by Stockport Corporation and inaugurated on 14 June 1968.

Plaque on Bunsall incline provided by the SLS and unveiled on 7 January 1973 *(John Marshall)*

The next section of the old CHPR track is a beautiful walk beside the Fernilee reservoir, which was begun in 1932 and inaugurated on 10 June 1937. Before this the railway ran on a shelf in the side of the valley. From the dam the track can be followed along a shelf above the river, past Folds End Farm to the overbridge filled in when the A5002 was straightened. The track continues on the other side of the road along a grassy embankment to the head of Shallcross incline, GR016796. Here there are remains of the reservoir and overgrown mounds of earth marking the site of the stationary engine house. The course of the incline is partly built over but an easy diversion to the left leads down to where it can be rejoined at GR015800 for a walk down the lower half which has been partially cleared.

The Shallcross yard area is now occupied by old peoples' homes, named 'Cromford Court'. The base of the old crane remains and also notices 'Shut and Fasten Gate' and 'Beware of Train'. Beyond the CHPR track has been made into a linear park by the local council. At the start of the path is a circular plaque with a reproduction of the seal of the CHPR in its centre, mounted in a circular stone surround. In front of it is secured a cast-iron fish-bellied rail. Whaley Bridge station to Shallcross yard track was removed during 1966.

Randall Carr Brook is crossed by a segmental stone arch. This and the Goyt are the only watercourses of any significance crossed by the CHPR in its whole length. Just beyond here, at ground level on the left, is milestone 32. Opposite is a point lever. A fine stone arch, with a flight of steps on the left, carries the A6 road over. The path ends where the connection from Whaley Bridge station joined the CHPR, GR011809. Note the 1/4 milepost and loading gauge. The bridge under the Buxton line has been filled in. A diversion here by road under the Buxton railway and right at the next road bridge brings us to the former level crossing, GR012812.

To the right the track bed is occupied by a contractor's yard; to the left it is once more made into a linear park. A short walk leads to the top of Whaley incline. The stationary engine and later horse capstan were in the space on the right. Several railway notices were restored, but were later vandalised. At the incline foot a branch to the right served a mill. The track continues over the Goyt by a bowstring girder bridge into Cheshire, and so reaches the terminus of the Peak Forest Canal. The warehouse here is dated 1832. The rails entered the doors on each side of the canal basin to form the northern terminus of the railway, just over 33 miles from Cromford, 239ft 6in above sea level and 39ft lower than the Cromford Canal.

NOTE

1. PRO RAIL 144/1 Letter No. 49.

Staff pose outside the weigh house at the foot of Shallcross incline circa 1890. *(G.D. Pepper collection)*

Early container traffic in Shallcross Yard circa 1890. *(G.D. Pepper collection)*

INDEX

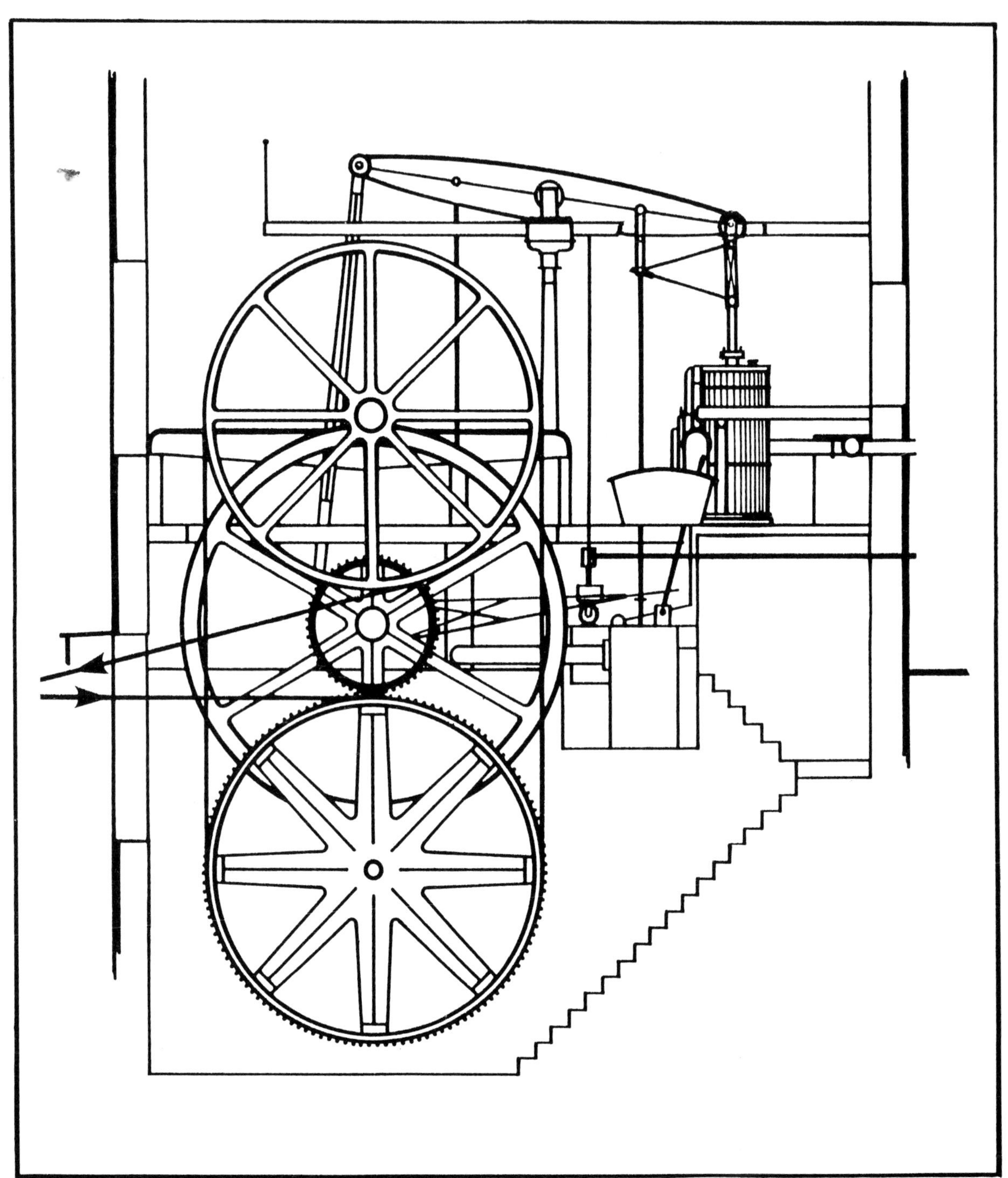

Side elevation of Middleton winding engine from an original drawing by M.W.I. Sissons